David takes tl [illegible]
Christians eith[illegible] understand or are intimidated to tackle in depth, and he makes it easily understood and practical in our daily walks with Christ. This book challenges us to address a side of God that many find uncomfortable in a way that is engaging and theologically sound.

— **Corey Trimble**, Lead Minister,
The Experience Community

In fifty-two years of ministry, I spent about half of that time serving North American churches and half in Africa serving Muslims. The numbers of new disciples we saw in America was a few hundred people, but in Africa it was a few hundred thousand, mostly disciples from Muslim backgrounds. The difference has been the toxic growth of humanistic worldviews that have over time mutated the biblical foundations of American and European churches.

One of the reasons that my wife and I became part of North Boulevard Church six years ago was David Young's hunger for a genuine a restoration of a biblical worldview that welcomes and embraces both the fruit and the gifts of the Holy Spirit. My wife and I have seen the fruit of disciples, demonstrating both character of Jesus, and a fruitfulness that only the Holy Spirit could produce.

David's book is a very winsome and valuable biblical survey of the Holy Spirit, which is, in tandem with much prayer, the foundation of any true disciple making momentum.

— **Jerry Trousdale**, author of *Miraculous Movements* and coauthor of *The Kingdom Unleashed*

There is a major dearth of information on the Holy Spirit in today's church. David Young has authored an outstanding volume examining the biblical doctrine of the Holy Spirit, his work, presence, and ministry in the lives of believers and church. I highly recommend this critical tool for serious preaching, teaching, and personal studying of this important topic. Don't miss the footnotes!

— **Dr. David Roadcup**, Professor of Discipleship, TCM International

David Young has done his readers a wonderful service in clearly identifying the Holy Spirit's work of pointing people to the Son, and of equipping Jesus' followers to accomplish His work. However, I must warn you that your traditional thinking most likely will be challenged!

— **John Caldwell**, DMin, longtime Senior Minister, Kingsway Christian Church

When I pick up a book by the preaching minister of North Boulevard Church of Christ on the Holy Spirit, I have to confess that my theological categories convince me that I know what it says. But David Young is not what you might think. His robust mind and contagious spirit create surprise after surprise as you turn the pages. Whether you agree with him or not, this book will take you on a journey that you won't regret. David challenges his own theological heritage with honesty, biblical integrity, and refreshing brevity to give us a simple, clear, and convincing perspective on the Spirit.

— **Roy Moran**, author of *Spent Matches* and Chairman of New Generations International

This small volume on the Holy Spirit answers in clear biblical language five most basic questions about the Spirit of God. And it shows why so many modern Christians have such a hard time with this central Christian doctrine. It is a gem! You won't find any short treatment of the Spirit better than this one!

— **Leonard Allen**, author of *Poured Out: The Spirit of God Empowering the Mission of God*

DAVID YOUNG

THE REAL LIFE THEOLOGY SERIES

HOLY SPIRIT

FILLED, EMPOWERED, AND LED

7

RENEW.org

Holy Spirit: Filled, Empowered, and Led

Requests for information should be sent via e-mail to Renew. Visit Renew.org for contact information.

Scripture quotations labeled AT are the author's own translation, in order to highlight precise features of the Bible's original languages.

Italics have been added to Scripture quotations by the author.

Any internet addresses (websites, blogs, etc.) in this book are offered as a resource. They are not intended in any way to be or imply an endorsement by Renew.org; nor does Renew.org vouch for the content of these sites and contact numbers for the life of this book.

ISBN (paperback) 978-1-949921-54-0
ISBN (Mobi) 978-1-949921-55-7
ISBN (ePub) 978-1-949921-56-4

Cover and interior design by Harrington Interactive Media (harringtoninteractive.com)

Printed in the United States of America

“Son of man, can these bones live?”

CONTENTS

GENERAL EDITORS' NOTE

The Bible teaches that we can know a person is saved or lost by the indwelling presence of the Holy Spirit in their life (Romans 8:9). At the heart of a disciple's life is walking in the Spirit. We are taught to be filled with the Spirit, led by the Spirit, and to keep in step with the Spirit. But what exactly is the Holy Spirit? How do we follow what the Bible teaches?

David Young is a trusted guide on the work of the Holy Spirit. He serves as the Lead Minister for the North Boulevard Church in Murfreesboro, Tennessee. He has worked for churches in Missouri, Kansas, and Tennessee, taught New Testament at several universities, and traveled widely as a teacher and preacher. He is the former host of the New Day Television Program, a board member for the Renew.org Network, and the author of several books, including *A New Day* (NB Press), *The Rhetoric of Jesus in the Gospel of Mark*

(Fortress Press, coauthored with Michael Strickland), *A Grand Illusion* (Renew.org), and *King Jesus and the Beauty of Obedience-Based Discipleship* (Zondervan). He holds multiple degrees in religion, including a PhD in New Testament from Vanderbilt University. David and his wife, Julie, have two married children.

This book expounds on the section from the Renew.org Leaders' Faith Statement called "The Holy Spirit":

> We believe God's desire is for everyone to be saved and come to the knowledge of the truth. Many hear the gospel but do not believe it because they are blinded by Satan and resist the pull of the Holy Spirit. We encourage everyone to listen to the Word and let the Holy Spirit convict them of their sin and draw them into a relationship with God through Jesus. We believe that when we are born again and indwelt by the Holy Spirit, we are to live as people who are filled, empowered, and led by the Holy Spirit. This is how we walk with God and discern his voice. A prayerful life, rich in the Holy Spirit, is fundamental to true discipleship and living in step with the kingdom reign of Jesus. We seek to be a prayerful, Spirit-led fellowship.

*See the full Network Faith Statements at the end of this book.

Support Scriptures: 1 Timothy 2:4; John 16:7–11; Acts 7:51; 1 John 2:20, 27; John 3:5; Ephesians 1:13–14; 5:18; Galatians 5:16–25; Romans 8:5–11; Acts 1:14; 2:42; 6:6; 9:40; 12:5; 13:3; 14:23; 20:36; 2 Corinthians 3:3.

The following tips might help you use this book more effectively (and the other books in the *Real Life Theology* series):

1. *Five questions, answers, and Scriptures.* We framed this book around five key questions with five short answers and five notable Scriptures. This format provides clarity, making it easier to commit crucial information to memory. This format also enables the books in the *Real Life Theology* series to support our catechism. Our catechism is a series of fixed questions and answers for instruction in church or home. In all, the series has fifty-two questions, answers, and key Scriptures. This particular book focuses on the five that are most pertinent to understanding the Holy Spirit.
2. *Personal reflection.* At the end of each chapter are six reflection questions. Each chapter is short and

intended for everyday people to read and then process. The questions help you to engage the specific teachings and, if you prefer, to journal your practical reflections.

3. *Discussion questions.* The reflection questions double as discussion-group questions. Even if you do not write down the answers, the questions can be used to stimulate group conversation.
4. *Summary videos.* You can find three to five-minute video teachings that summarize the book, as well as each chapter, at Renew.org. These short videos can function as standalone teachings. But for groups or group leaders using the book, they can also be used to launch discussion of the reading.

May God use this book to fuel faithful and effective disciple making in your life and church.

For King Jesus,
Bobby Harrington and Daniel McCoy
General Editors, *Real Life Theology* series

INTRODUCTION

> The great human dogma, then, is that the wind moves the trees. The great human heresy is that the trees move the wind.
> — G. K. Chesterton

Years ago, I came to the unhappy conclusion that many of us don't understand the Holy Spirit because we really don't want to. He is too wild, unpredictable, untamed, full of power, risky, unsettling, disruptive, and challenging. We prefer a domesticated faith, where our comfort is never upended by his power.

So if your church had two classrooms in its hallway, one labeled "The Study of the Holy Spirit" and the other labeled "The Holy Spirit Is Here," many of us would choose the former. We'd rather *study* the Holy Spirit than *experience* him. We like having a theology of the Spirit, but we are hesitant to embrace the real thing.

This is the story of many in the Western church: literally equipped with the best resources the church has ever possessed, many of us fear the one resource that can actually change the world—the Holy Spirit.

The early church exploded in growth not because they had fancy mission statements and programs. The early church exploded in growth because they had the power of the Holy Spirit. Imagine a church whose strategic vision looked like this:

> I will pour out my Spirit on all people. . . . I will show wonders in the heavens above and signs on the earth below, blood and fire and billows of smoke. The sun will be turned to darkness and the moon to blood before the coming of the great and glorious day of the Lord. And everyone who calls on the name of the Lord will be saved. (Acts 2:17–21)

Blood and fire and billows of smoke. This is the vision God has planned for you. This is the power of the Holy Spirit. It's not merely a matter of having the right doctrine. It's rather a matter of experiencing the Spirit himself. If I could accomplish one thing in this book, it would be to convince you to stop quenching the Spirit's fire and start experiencing his power.

So who is the Holy Spirit and what does he want to do in me?

Questions about the Holy Spirit have been around ever since Paul was told by the disciples of John the Baptist that "we have not even heard that there is a Holy Spirit" (Acts 19:2). Our many questions about the Holy Spirit arise for three reasons. First, the Spirit is God, and because God is so much bigger than we are, there will always remain questions about what the powerful Spirit is doing.

Second, the church has often argued about the Spirit. We've argued over such things as the relationship of the Spirit to the Father and Son, how believers get the Spirit, and whether or not the gifts of the Spirit are still available. These conflicts have sometimes left the typical follower of Jesus so confused they just ignore the Spirit altogether.

Third, many questions about the Spirit arise because the secular worldview meticulously cultivated in the Western world over the last half-millennium has left many of us bereft of *any* real spiritual awareness at all. Unable to discern deeply the presence of *anything* spiritual leaves us ill-equipped to understand the work of the most powerful of spirits—the Holy Spirit.

With this book, I seek to answer five of the most fundamental questions believers bring to the subject of the Holy Spirit:

- What is a spirit?
- How does the Holy Spirit move us toward Jesus?
- What does it mean for the Holy Spirit to live within us?
- How does the Holy Spirit make us like Jesus?
- How do we seek the Holy Spirit's leadership in our lives?

These comprise the five chapters of this book.

Before beginning, however, let's point out that the picture of the Spirit in the Bible is an evolving picture, coming into clear focus only when seen through Jesus Christ, and even then, most clearly when explained in the works of John and Paul.

In the earliest portions of Scripture, the Spirit is a dynamic and, at times, unpredictable power who personifies God's movements within the creation. In the first half of the Bible, the Spirit hardly appears as a person at all, but rather as a powerful force—like a mighty wind. In the latter pages of the Old Testament, the Spirit begins to function in a more rational role and is frequently assigned the very specific task of inspiring prophetic speech. And in these latter pages, many of the prophetic oracles tell us that the Spirit will be characteristic of Jesus' ministry and the new covenant in its entirety.

In the New Testament, the Spirit does indeed characterize the messianic ministry of Jesus, providing power and direction for his work. The Synoptic Gospels—Matthew, Mark, and Luke—show that Jesus was led by the Spirit, and the Spirit still appears more as a power than as a person in the Synoptic Gospels. In the book of Acts, the same power is offered to all believers, since all believers are now offered the Holy Spirit, who brings divine power to the church.

In John's Gospel, however, we see that the Spirit is more than just a power, but is actually a person—distinct from the Father and the Son, but one with them. His personhood has been true all along, but we see it more clearly in John. Though John still uses the neuter pronoun to describe the Spirit, he speaks of the Spirit as a person.[1] John continues to present the Spirit as providing power for the believers, but he goes further. For John, as we'll discover in what follows, the Spirit is a person who provides a new way of living. We are born of the Spirit, he explains. We worship in the Spirit. And the Spirit actually represents a new way of life, distinguished from that of mere flesh.

In the works of Paul, the fullest image of the Spirit in the Bible emerges. There we learn that the Spirit is the very air that Christians are to breathe—that we are to live in the Spirit, to be led by the Spirit, and to be sanctified by the Spirit. This last phrase sums up the work of the Spirit for the disciple. As the divine and personal presence of a powerful and holy God, the Spirit's main task in the Christian's life is to empower us to become like Jesus. The Spirit himself forms a new way of living for the believers. He is our new DNA in Christ, changing us into the likeness of Jesus at a core level.

THE SPIRIT'S MAIN TASK IN THE CHRISTIAN'S LIFE IS TO EMPOWER US TO BECOME LIKE JESUS.

Let's take the five questions relevant to this work and seek their biblical answers. As you continue reading, however, please remember that our ultimate goal is not simply to develop a doctrine about the Holy Spirit. Our ultimate goal that extends out of a renewed understanding of the Spirit is to have an immersive experience of the Spirit. Don't settle for merely knowing *about* the Spirit. Seek instead to *know* the Spirit and to *live* in him.

1

WHAT IS A SPIRIT?

Answer: A spirit is a personal being, with rational, emotional, and volitional capacities, who transcends the known physical world but also acts within it.

God is spirit, and his worshipers must worship in the Spirit and in truth.
— John 4:24

We've all seen holograms: those images of dogs, doves, and people that seem to move as you turn the picture. Holograms are fascinating because they present what's called "parallax"—the quality that makes the foreground move differently from the background, changing the actual image as you turn the hologram and making the image appear to have life.

How does this work? Well, I'll leave the explanation to the laser physicists and simply point out that we are not attracted to holograms because of the physics behind them. Rather, we are attracted to holograms because they simulate real-life movement. We are drawn to life, not to mere explanations of life. So it is with the Spirit.

HOW AND WHY

Science can explain the *how* of life—how chemicals interact in nature, in the human body, and in the universe—but science cannot explain *why* they do: Why is there matter? Why is there a universe? Why is there life? Why do we do the things we do? These are spiritual questions—questions about *why* life springs out of matter to end up thinking, reasoning, imagining, loving, and hoping. The entire 500-year scientific enterprise of the West has mistakenly believed that if we can explain *how* something happens, we have also explained *why* it happens. But the two questions are completely different.

If you lost your keys in the garage, you don't look for them in the kitchen simply because the lighting is better there. In the same way, looking for *how* a mixture of warm and cold air can create a storm doesn't explain *why* warm and cold mix in the first place. Explaining how a woman remembers to bring her purse does not explain why she remembers. Explaining how a community seeks justice does not explain why it does. Explaining how the brain functions does not explain why it does. A chemical or electrical reaction in the brain can be measured in a machine. A thought cannot.

To answer *why* questions, we must think in spiritual categories, which in fact we all do, whether we realize it or not. Rationality is not a mere chemical question; it is primarily a spiritual one. Justice is not a question merely for biologists; it is a question for all humans. And God is not a matter of particle physics; he is spirit and from his Spirit comes every particle.

Spirit is the *why*-force behind every *how*-answer in the universe. Embedded in all of reality is a spiritual dimension distinct from physics but forming a sort of fabric in which all of physics operates. This spiritual fabric is the animating force that keeps the universe orderly. It is the reason for gravity, for electromagnetism, for waves, particles,

SPIRIT IS THE *WHY*-FORCE BEHIND EVERY *HOW*-ANSWER IN THE UNIVERSE.

purposes, intentions, plans, aspirations, and personhood. So even if you could gather organic matter matching every single molecule found in a human body and piece it together in a lab, it still wouldn't be alive, for life is not just the sum of the chemicals in a person's body. Life is that which is behind the chemicals in the body—it is the force, the energy, the person, who makes the chemicals breathe, act, and reason. It is spirit that makes us live. Chemicals are necessary, but without spirit, they are dead. Without spirit, they wouldn't even exist at all.

THE SPIRITUAL BEHIND THE PHYSICAL

Let me put it another way. If you could pull back the curtains on the visible universe—that part of creation that scientists study—you would see a deeper, spiritual reality behind the physical. You would see a world of personal forces animating the universe, giving it its purpose: now creating, now resting, now wrestling, now luring, now calming. You would see angels and demons. You would see the meaning of the universe (its *why*) and not just the mechanics of the universe (its *how*). You would see everything that is spiritual.

The book of Revelation bears this out graphically. Behind every earthquake in Revelation is a spiritual decision made in heaven. Behind persecution are evil spirits. Behind the rise and collapse of empires are spirits in mortal combat. And behind every person's life is a spirit—an immaterial, rational, individual person-animating life. In this sense, one's spirit is almost like one's life itself: that mysterious force that makes the two plus two of mere matter equal the five of a living person. When used in the sense of "life," the Bible can occasionally speak of even animals as having "spirit"—that is, "life" (see Ecclesiastes 3:19).

Behind the curtain of the visible universe is an entire world of the spiritual. It is analogous to the way that a movie screen shows a mere projection of real actors filmed a year before it ever entered the theater. If the movie is good, even though it is composed only of pixels on a screen, it elicits real emotions. That's because behind the projection lie real people who actually generated the feelings, who live and breathe and themselves have feelings. In the same way, behind every single physical phenomenon is a spiritual force animating and empowering it.

This mystical dimension of the universe explains why the cluster of terms in the Bible typically translated "soul" and "spirit" are connected to ideas of wind, breath, and life. In the Hebrew Bible, the typical terms are *ruach* and *nephesh*. The former sometimes means "wind"—that unseen force that moves the trees and cools the skin. We cannot see the wind, but we can see that there is wind. The latter Hebrew term sometimes means life—the breath that makes matter think, plan, and create.[2] We cannot see life, but we can see that there is life, just as we can see the tragedy of the end of life.

This interpretation of reality is also presented in the New Testament, often using the words *pneuma* and *psyche*.[3] These terms derive their meaning from concepts of wind, breath, and one's rational, emotional, and volitional capacities. To see the spiritual is to see behind (or within) the physical—to perceive the ultimate and animating power that generates the physical.

If we want a rich experience of the Holy Spirit, it is imperative that we recover a sense of what a spirit is. Many of us fail to have a rich experience of the Holy Spirit because we are unaware that there are such things as spirits at all. But spirits are real. They are all around us, and we *already* follow one spirit or another.

THE SPIRIT AND THE BODY

Spirits are metaphysical persons (that is, persons who transcend our experience of physics). They have individuality and volition. They think, feel, and act—both above and within creation. They include angels, spiritual beings who are charged with doing God's will both in heaven and on earth (see Hebrews 12:4). They also include the devil and his demons (Revelation 16:14). Spirits inhabit the ethereal realm (Ephesians 2:2) and constitute the powers of the unseen world (Ephesians 6:11–12; Colossians 2:20). Though they may appear in bodily form, they are essentially otherworldly in nature (Luke 24:39). Hence, both John and Paul frequently make contrasts between *flesh* and *spirit* (see John 3:6; 6:63; Romans 8:5; Philippians 3:3).

All humans possess a "spirit." The spirit is that inner part of a person that gives life and is inherently related to God. A person's spirit is their conscious essence—something like one's mind. In some ways, the spirit is what we mean when we say "I" or "me"—as opposed to "my." So we can say things like, "I (the spirit) *have* two legs (the body)." We instinctively know our spirits and bodies are not the same thing. We can *know* with our spirit (1 Corinthians 2:11), *rejoice* in our spirit (Luke 1:47), be *anguished* in our spirit (Job 7:11), be *refreshed* in our spirit (1 Corinthians 16:18), and *worship* with our spirit (John 4:24; 1 Corinthians 14:15). A person's spirit lives on after that person's body is dead (1 Samuel 28:13–14; 1 Corinthians 5:5; 14:16; Hebrews 12:23).

RECOVERING THE SPIRIT

In order to understand and fully experience the Holy Spirit, we must recover a spiritual view of the creation. I say "recover" because there was once a time (and still is in much of the world) when humans naturally perceived spiritual realities. We knew that the world is, to borrow a concept from Canadian philosopher Charles Taylor's often-quoted *A Secular Age*, enchanted—that there is a "ghost in the machine" of creation animating and enlivening it.[4] That's why, Taylor explains, most of history's populations could not imagine a world without God and spirits. Rather than asking whether or not the Holy Spirit exists, most of the world would naturally ask, "Which spirit exists here?" But in the West, where we have settled for *how* questions instead of *why* questions, we have lost much of our sense of enchantment. So we are left asking the impoverished question, "Is there a spirit at all?"

To understand the Holy Spirit, we must first comprehend the spiritual realities behind, or beneath, or within our daily lives. Indeed, comprehending the meaning of "spirit" is half the game in understanding the Holy Spirit. The problem so many Western churches have with the Holy Spirit is not really theological; it is cultural. Our culture struggles to understand *anything* spiritual, so when we speak of "the Holy Spirit," we don't have a category for him. We are like a man writing a book on how it feels to have a baby. He can say anything he wants, of course, but we all know that he really has no idea what he's talking about. In the same way, people

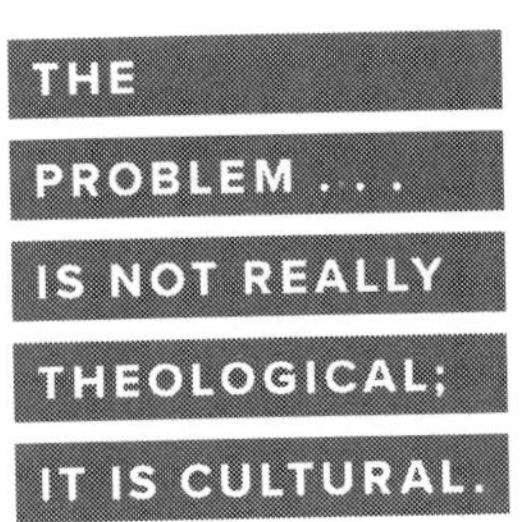

who do not live aware of the spiritual dimension of life cannot understand the Holy Spirit. But when we awaken to God's Spirit in our spirit, we gain the necessary language for discerning his presence. We begin to have an experience of the Spirit that enriches our lives.

Since the Spirit is everywhere, in order to see his work, we don't have to look elsewhere. Rather, we have to look more deeply at what's already before us. Rather than seeing our lives as a set of random coincidences, we learn to see that there is a purpose and design to them. Rather than seeing loneliness as a mere state of mind, we learn to see it as the howl of our spirits against their separation from God. Rather than seeing the rise and fall of nations as the mere result of social and political changes, we learn to see the spiritual war behind physical war, with God directing all of history for the sake of his ultimate victory. Rather than seeing mere physics behind the growth of grass, the food on our table, and the loves in our lives, we learn to see the power of God behind each of these. We must learn to see that the spiritual is behind everything physical. *Everything.*

As we develop a biblical theology of the Holy Spirit, don't forget that the first step is to recognize the spiritual depths of creation. It's only then that we can understand this, the third member of the Holy Trinity. It's only then that we can experience the fullness of the power of the Holy Spirit.

REFLECTION & DISCUSSION QUESTIONS

1. If you had two classrooms, one labeled "The Study of the Holy Spirit" and the other "The Holy Spirit Is Here," which one would you be more comfortable entering and why?

2. If someone asked you what a spirit is, how would you answer?

3. Unlike many other cultures around the world, North American culture does not put much stock in spirits. What are some negative effects that follow when a culture stops believing in the spiritual realm?

4. In your church experience so far, how much emphasis has been placed on spirits (good or evil), and how has that affected your perspective?

5. If you fully lived with the belief that both angels and demons exist in the spiritual realm, how might that alter how you process the events that go on in your life?

6. Read Ephesians 6:12. This passage describes how our fight is against the spiritual forces of evil. Can you describe a battle you have faced before that was ultimately against spiritual forces?

2

HOW DOES THE HOLY SPIRIT MOVE US TOWARD JESUS?

Answer: The Holy Spirit moves us toward Jesus through the Word, through his power, and through deep conviction.

For we know, brothers and sisters loved by God, that he has chosen you, because our gospel came to you not simply with words but also with power, with the Holy Spirit and deep conviction. You know how we lived among you for your sake.
— 1 Thessalonians 1:4–5

The Spirit of God is the creative power and the life-giving essence of God.[5] The Holy Spirit is the personal force of God beneath, behind, and within the universe that holds it all together and gives it its purpose. God himself is a spirit (John 4:24), but he also *has* a Spirit—who is one person of the Trinity—distinct from the Father and the Son yet also completely one with them. The Spirit is above us, beneath us, around us, and if you are a believer in Jesus, within you. He is the presence of God hovering over creation. He animates the universe, motivates it, and shapes it. He is the life-giving and world-transforming presence of God, permeating every crevice of creation. As the psalmist writes, "Whither shall I go from thy spirit?" (Psalm 139:7, KJV).

But the Spirit does not point to himself. Rather, the Spirit's work is to point us to Jesus (John 15:26). He is very unselfish. And so our primary interest in the Holy Spirit should always be motivated by a desire to become like Jesus. It's worth remembering that the Holy Spirit has no name; he points to the one named Jesus.

So how does this Spirit draw us to Jesus? Even more deeply, why is it necessary for the Spirit to draw us to him? Couldn't we just choose Jesus on our own volition?

Paul's comment to the Thessalonian church gives us a short answer for how the Spirit draws us toward Jesus. Speaking of his experience with the Thessalonians, Paul says, "For we know, brothers and sisters loved by God, that he has chosen you, because our gospel came to you not simply with words but also with power, with the Holy Spirit and deep conviction" (1 Thessalonians 1:4–5). The Spirit works through the Word, through his power, and through deep conviction.

These works of the Spirit are necessary because none of us can come to Jesus on our own. Jesus plainly says it: "No one can come to me unless the Father has enabled them" (John 6:65). Paul puts it this way: "For who knows a person's thoughts except their own spirit within them? In the same way no one knows the thoughts of God except the Spirit of God" (1 Corinthians 2:11). In order to see the spiritual things of God, we require the Spirit of God. "As the heavens are higher than the earth, so are my ways higher than your ways and my thoughts than your thoughts," says the Lord (Isaiah 55:9). We need the Spirit to draw us to God because only the Spirit fully knows the will of God.

There is another reason, however, that we need the Spirit to draw us to God: we are hopelessly plunged in sin and are simply too broken by sin to come to God without his drawing power. Our purposes are selfish. Our desires are disordered. And worst of all, our will is broken. Blinded by our sin, we do not have sufficient power to draw ourselves to God. To quote Paul again, "The god of this age has blinded the minds of unbelievers, so that they cannot see the light of the gospel that displays the glory of Christ, who is the image of God" (2 Corinthians 4:4). We are like the GPS on our phones when the battery is dead. No matter how much we might think we can navigate our lives toward God, we don't have the power to do it.

So God uses his Spirit to draw us to him through Jesus.

How does the Spirit do this? Using 1 Thessalonians 1:4–5 as a key passage, let's explore three ways.

THE WORD

THE FIRST WAY THE Spirit draws us to God is through the Word of God. In the Old Testament, the Spirit gave physical strength, executive prowess, and engineering skills to various individuals. But he also gave them the very words of God. The Spirit has a rational function—that of communicating the specifics of God's will to humans. In the prophetic works of the Old Testament, the Spirit is frequently described as revealing the details of God's will. He inspired the prophets to communicate the exact message of God. He inspired the writing of the Bible.

This is claimed by the Old Testament writers themselves.

- “But the Spirit of God came even on him, and he walked along prophesying” (1 Samuel 19:23).
- “Then the Spirit of God came on Zechariah son of Jehoiada the priest. He stood before the people and said, ‘This is what God says’” (2 Chronicles 24:20).
- “My Spirit, who is on you, will not depart from you, and my words that I have put in your mouth will always be on your lips” (Isaiah 59:21).
- “Then the Spirit of the Lord came on me, and he told me to say” (Ezekiel 11:5).
- “They made their hearts as hard as flint and would not listen to the law or to the words that the Lord Almighty had sent by his Spirit through the earlier prophets” (Zechariah 7:12).

The Old Testament writers were inspired by the Spirit of God to record the things they wrote.

In the New Testament, the Spirit’s inspiration of the Old Testament is explicitly maintained over and over again. Jesus affirmed the authority of the Old Testament saying, for example, that not a single dot or line of the Old Testament should be broken (Matthew 5:17–20). The book of Acts declares that the Old Testament came by the Holy Spirit (Acts 1:16; 4:25). Paul pronounces the law to be holy, righteous, and good (Romans 7:12).

In the same way, Jesus promised the apostles that the Spirit would guide them in the truth that’s preserved for us in the New Testament (John 14:26; 15:26; 16:13; 16:15). Paul claims to have spoken the very words of God because, as he explains, he has the Spirit of God (1 Corinthians 14:37). Paul points out that God's Word has "now been revealed by the Spirit to God's holy apostles and prophets" (Ephesians 3:5). The Scriptures are fully trustworthy because they are "God-breathed," a term that literally means "Spirited-of-God" (2 Timothy 3:16–17). The Word of God is described as the Spirit's sword (Ephesians 6:17). Peter says that the Scripture came to us by prophets who were moved by the Holy Spirit (2 Peter 1:21).

We do not come to God merely by looking deeply within our own selves. We require specific instruction in order to follow Jesus. Without the Word, we would not even know who Jesus is! This is why the functions of the Word of God and those of the Spirit are often described in the same language in Scripture. Here are a few examples:

Function	Spirit	Word
Creating	Genesis 1:2	Hebrews 1:3; 2 Peter 3:5
Giving new birth	John 3:8	1 Peter 1:23–25
Giving life	2 Corinthians 3:6	James 1:18
Purifying	Titus 3:5	James 1:21
Sanctifying	1 Corinthians 6:11	2 Thessalonians 2:13
Indwelling	Romans 8:11	Colossians 3:16
Bearing truth	1 John 5:7	John 17:17

When we read the Word of God, we are listening to the Spirit's voice. In this way, the Word is a primary way the Spirit draws us to God. The Spirit draws us to Jesus, in part, through the Word of God.

SIGNS, WONDERS, AND POWERS

SECOND, THE SPIRIT DRAWS us to God through what the Bible typically calls signs, wonders, and powers (see 1 Corinthians 2:4–5; Ephesians 3:16–29). Whereas the Word gives us very specific instructions for how to approach God, the Spirit often provides signs, wonders, and powers in order to confirm to us the Word of God. The Word constitutes a specific and rational form of revelation. Signs, wonders, and powers constitute a general form of revelation that can transcend rational knowledge.

THE SPIRIT OFTEN PROVIDES SIGNS, WONDERS, AND POWERS TO CONFIRM TO US THE WORD OF GOD.

Many Christians, including myself, grew up in churches that held cessationist views of miracles—that is, we were taught that God doesn't do miracles anymore. Defining miracles as "things contrary to the laws of nature," we came to believe that God ceased doing things contrary to the laws of nature after the first century (hence the term "cessationist"). But we should know that this definition of miracles is not biblical, but was rather bequeathed to us by the Enlightenment philosopher David Hume, who was an agnostic. Using Hume's Enlightenment definitions, many of us were taught that the most we could hope for was "providence," which we defined as God working *through* the laws of nature.

Beholden to Hume's definitions, many of us are left with the impoverished view that God does almost nothing in our daily lives—so we experience very little of the power that the Holy Spirit offers. We are left with mere doctrines about the Spirit. Where are the blood, the fire, and the billows of smoke? In the Bible, we do not find Hume's definition of miracles. Rather, we learn that the Spirit performs all kinds of signs, wonders, and powers all of the time (whether contrary to or through the so-called "laws of nature"). In the Bible we are invited to a better definition of miracles, namely, that God acts among us in significant, powerful, or wonderful ways.

For example, the Bible calls the rainbow a "sign." It is a physical phenomenon that springs from and points to a spiritual reality. The rainbow is a sign that God will never destroy the earth by flood again. When we see a rainbow, we see a "sign" from God demonstrating his faithfulness. And such signs have not ceased. God has been performing signs since the beginning of creation, in fact, and he will never stop performing them. To miss this spiritual reality is to miss the point of the rainbow, no matter how much you understand about photons, air mass wavelengths, and receptor cells.

The Spirit places all kinds of signs before us—people of influence and natural phenomena, such as mountain vistas and terrifying storms. He places intimate signs before us, such as joy or even sickness. In each case, the Spirit is using physical phenomena to point us to spiritual realities, thereby drawing us to God. The intense human desire to receive justice is, for example, a sign that God wants us to live in his image, since he is a just God.

The same can be said of wonders and powers. The Bible does not distinguish between things done "contrary to nature" and things done "through nature" as we do today. Rather, the Bible simply affirms that God has always done powerful and wonderful things. The Spirit still uses wonders and powers to draw us to God. This is not complicated: when God gives us a gift that makes our jaws drop, that's a "wonder," and when God provides us with the resources we need in order to do something he wants, that's a "power."

At times, God's powers and wonders are so big that they defy physical explanation—such as when Jesus walked on water (Matthew 14:23–33) or when Peter raised Dorcas from the dead (Acts 9:36–43). God has often performed such physics-defying feats, and the book of Revelation indicates that God has not stopped doing these. He still does, at his discretion, such physics-defying wonders and powers. He still heals the sick, enables people to walk across water, and raises the dead. Just because these are not common in our part of the world doesn't mean they don't happen. There are numerous testimonies from reliable people all over the world that God is still doing such things, and I have personally seen such powers and wonders.[6]

At other times, however, God does less extraordinary wonders and powers—such as offering us peace during the storms of life, supplying us with people who love us, encouraging us through his church, and much more. Remember, *everything* has a spiritual dimension, and *everything* truly good comes from God.

We've been conditioned by our modern world to say that it's only a miracle when two plus three equals six. But another form of miracle occurs when two plus three equals five, even though we had neither the two nor the three necessary to get the five. God does this all the time! He is always performing signs, wonders, and powers in this sense.

Such signs, wonders, and powers are meant to draw us to Jesus. Here's how John puts it: "Jesus performed many other signs in the presence of his disciples, which are not recorded in this book. But these are written that you may believe that Jesus is the Messiah, the Son of God, and that by believing you may have life in his name" (John 20:30–31). Mark says it this way: "Then the disciples went out and preached everywhere, and the Lord worked with them and confirmed his word by the signs that accompanied it" (Mark 16:20).

So the second way the Spirit draws us to God is through the constant use of signs, wonders, and powers. To experience the work of the Spirit is to open our eyes to his power among us. It is to see and give credit to the Spirit for what he is already doing in your life—works that your theology may have caused you to miss. It is to stop using the word "luck," and to start speaking of the power of the Spirit of God in everything good that happens in life.

CONVICTION

It is not enough to have a written text of the Bible, and signs, wonders, and powers alone won't convict sinners. The Jewish people in Jesus' day had a written text that was inspired by the Holy Spirit, and they witnessed many miracles. But that was not enough. "The letter kills," Paul explains, "but the Spirit gives life" (2 Corinthians 3:6). So the Holy Spirit does more than merely give us an inspired book or perform miracles.

He personally convicts our hearts so we can believe and obey God.

This is what the prophet Ezekiel promised about the coming of Jesus: "And I will put my Spirit in you and move you to follow my decrees and be careful to keep my laws" (Ezekiel 36:27). Note that in this text the Spirit works consistently with the Word of God, but apart from it too. This was also the case for Lydia. When Paul preached the Word to her, "The Lord opened her heart to respond to Paul's message" (Acts 16:14). Note that there is a twofold work of the Spirit in this text: the proclamation of the Word *and* the opening of the heart.

God gives us the written Word, but we require the movement of the Spirit in order to obey it. We are simply too sinful to make fully good choices on our own, so the Spirit moves our hearts to say *yes*. The work of the Spirit includes knowledge, but it also *transcends knowledge*: "Out of his glorious riches he may strengthen you with power through his Spirit in your inner being . . . to know this love that *surpasses knowledge*" (Ephesians 3:16–19).

GOD GIVES US THE WRITTEN WORD, BUT WE REQUIRE THE MOVEMENT OF THE SPIRIT IN ORDER TO OBEY IT.

Perhaps this convicting work of the Spirit is what is meant in other texts where we read of hearts being moved by God. God moved the heart of Cyrus and of Ezra (2 Chronicles 36:22; Ezra 1:5). God puts things on the hearts of David, Nehemiah, and Titus (1 Chronicles 28:12; Ezra 1:1; Nehemiah 2:12; 7:5; 2 Corinthians 8:16). The phrase "moving the heart" seems to describe the Spirit impressing truth in a new or persuasive way in the mind of the listener. When the phrase is used in Ezra and Nehemiah, the Lord is not revealing new truths but opening up the hearts of those who already have his truth to see its full implications.

So how does the Spirit convict our hearts? We sense the voice of God within our human spirit. It is a quiet, prompting voice by which God seeks to lead, guide, and fill us (Galatians 5:18; 5:25; Ephesians 5:18). It is resistible because Scripture describes people resisting the Spirit (Acts 7:51). But by his personal presence, the Spirit will lead us and guide us and impress on us things that only come from God. Paul's prayer about the convicting work of the Spirit is thrilling yet somewhat mystical: "that the eyes of your heart may be enlightened in order that you may know the hope to which he has called you" (Ephesians 1:18). Perhaps it is enough to say that when you feel convicted to obey the Word of God, that's the Holy Spirit.

One more word about how the Holy Spirit moves in us. We must be cautious about the convicting work of the Spirit, for there are other spirits who want to convict us as well (1 John 4:1). These false spirits encourage us to follow our own sentiments and to label them the work of the Spirit. We should always test our feelings by consulting other believers and the Scriptures themselves. There are few dangers greater than confusing our thoughts with the thoughts of the Spirit.[7]

However we are drawn to Jesus, we must affirm that we require the Spirit's movement in our hearts in order to be drawn.

REFLECTION & DISCUSSION QUESTIONS

1. We cannot ultimately defeat sin and draw close to God without the Holy Spirit, but most of us have tried to. Can you describe a struggle in your life where you should have depended more on the power of the Spirit?

2. Read 1 Thessalonians 1:4–5. Paul states that the Holy Spirit moves us toward Jesus through the Word, through his power, and through deep conviction. How would you explain each of these to a new believer?

3. How does knowing that the Scriptures are "God-breathed" (meaning "Spirited-of-God") and that the Spirit is described as revealing the details of God's will enhance your reading of God's Word?

4. This chapter defines "miracles" as whenever God acts among us in significant, powerful, or wonderful ways. How does this biblical definition of miracles change how you might have seen miraculous wonders in your own life? Describe some.

5. Describe a time in your life when the Spirit personally convicted you, and then gave you the power to obey God.

6. We are called to love the unlovable and to forgive the unforgivable, but this can only be done through the power of the Spirit. How has this been reflected—or how could this be reflected—in your life?

3

WHAT DOES IT MEAN FOR THE HOLY SPIRIT TO LIVE WITHIN US?

Answer: The Spirit lives within us by immersing us in a relationship with God and by transforming us into the image of Christ.

And we all, who with unveiled faces contemplate
the Lord's glory, are being transformed into
his image with ever-increasing glory, which
comes from the Lord, who is the Spirit.
— 2 Corinthians 3:18

The Holy Spirit is everywhere at all times because he is God. This is implied in the opening verses of the Bible, where the Spirit of God is described as hovering over creation (Genesis 1:2). In a special sense, however, the Holy Spirit lives within us as believers. The Old Testament prophets had promised that the Spirit would be widely available to the people of God in these last days (Isaiah 44:3–4; Joel 2:28–29; Ezekiel 37:1–14). John the Baptist preached that though his baptism was in water Jesus would baptize his followers in the Holy Spirit (Matthew 3:11). Jesus himself promised the disciples that they would receive the Spirit whom "the world cannot receive" (John 14:17, KJV). And Peter announced that the Spirit is given to all who obey Christ (Acts 5:32). The rest of the New Testament indicates that having the Spirit within us is a mark that we belong to Christ and are separate from the world (Romans 8:11; 1 Corinthians 6:19; Galatians 5:18; 2 Timothy 1:14). As Paul says, "Because you are his sons, God sent the Spirit of his Son into our hearts, the Spirit who calls out, 'Abba, Father'" (Galatians 4:6).

So what does it mean for the Spirit to live within those of us who believe?

THE SPIRIT PROVIDES US AN IMMERSIVE EXPERIENCE IN GOD

Let's start by describing the normative way that believers receive the Holy Spirit: through faith in Christ.[8] Jesus promised that the Spirit would be given to those who believe: "'Whoever believes in me, as Scripture has said, rivers of living water will flow from within them.' By this he meant the Spirit, whom those who believed in him were later to receive" (John 7:38–39). This is also what Paul affirms in his rhetorical question to the Galatians: "Did you receive the Spirit by the works of the law, or by believing what you heard?" (Galatians 3:2). He goes on: "He redeemed us in order that the blessing given to Abraham might come to the Gentiles through Christ Jesus, so that *by faith* we might receive the promise of the Spirit" (Galatians 3:14).

In the same way that we receive the indwelling Father and Son upon our profession of faith, we also receive the Holy Spirit (see also Ephesians 3:17; John 14:23).

There are several important metaphors for our reception of the Spirit that are used in Scripture. One is that of new birth. Jesus puts it this way: "Very truly I tell you, no one can enter the kingdom of God unless they are born of water and the Spirit. Flesh gives birth to flesh, but the Spirit gives birth to spirit" (John 3:5–6). The idea Jesus presents here is that our conversion changes our very nature from that of what he calls "the flesh" to that of the Spirit. To receive the Spirit is to adopt a new mode of living that is different from that of the world—to live by spiritual means rather than by the bodily lusts. This is why the Bible can say that we are made alive *through* the Spirit (John 6:63; Romans 8:2). Real life is not the life of lusts and bodily pleasures. Real life is spiritual life in Christ. When we are born of the Spirit, we become God's children, and the Spirit himself testifies that we now belong to God (Romans 8:16; Galatians 4:6).

We should not neglect the reference to water in John 3, since baptism provides a second metaphor for our reception of the Holy Spirit. John the Baptist had promised that Jesus would baptize believers in the Holy Spirit. Just prior to his ascension, Jesus told the disciples to remain in Jerusalem until they received this promised Holy Spirit. Then in Acts 2, the disciples received the outpouring of the Spirit and used the occasion to preach the first sermon about the resurrected Jesus. They concluded the sermon by promising all who repented and were baptized that they too would receive the Holy Spirit: "The promise is for you and your children and for all who are far off—for all whom the Lord our God will call" (Acts 2:39). The Bible links water baptism to an immersion in the Holy Spirit. Just as believers are baptized in water to wash away sins, so we are baptized in the Spirit to become new creatures, typically at the same time (Acts 22:16).[9]

This explains why Jesus' final words in Matthew 28:18–20 include the command for the disciples to baptize *into* the name of the Father, the Son, and the Holy Spirit (AT). The word "into" (*eis* in Greek) does not mean "by the authority of" but rather "into a relationship with." Jesus' command for us to baptize "into the name of the Spirit" implies that baptism is the point at which we enter a relationship with the Spirit. So when Paul is urging Christian unity, he refers to our Holy Spirit baptism: "For we were all baptized by one Spirit so as to form one body—whether Jews or Gentiles, slave or free—and we were all given the one Spirit to drink" (1 Corinthians 12:13). And when speaking of our salvation, Paul says, "He saved us through the washing of rebirth and renewal by the Holy Spirit, whom he poured out on us generously through Jesus Christ our Savior" (Titus 3:5–6).

To say that we are "baptized in the Spirit" is to say that at the moment of our justification, we are offered an immersive experience in the Spirit of God. No wonder he is called a gift (Acts 2:38–39)! Faith accompanied by water baptism constitutes the normative way that we receive the Holy Spirit.[10]

THE SPIRIT TRANSFORMS US INTO THE IMAGE OF CHRIST

So we receive the Spirit when we respond in faith to Jesus Christ—typically at the point of our water baptism. But what is the role of the Spirit in our lives? In the next chapter, we'll look at some ways that the Spirit equips us for the work of Jesus, but here, let's explore the most fundamental work of the Spirit: he transforms us into the image of Jesus. In fact, transformation is the real essence of the Spirit's work. Everywhere we read of him in the Bible, the Spirit is working to effect a transformation of God's creation or of God's people. This is true in the historical sections of the Old Testament, where the Spirit occasionally appears as an undefined power—at times even an event—who dynamically swept down upon persons to accomplish God's will. This is also true in the prophetic passages of the Old Testament, where the Spirit was more rational and functioned to give knowledge to the people of God. And it is true in the writings of Paul, where we learn that the Spirit's very substance provides the realm for a new existence for disciples of Christ. In each case, the Spirit works to transform the creation according to God's will.

TRANSFORMATION IS THE REAL ESSENCE OF THE SPIRIT'S WORK.

Paul describes the transformational role of the Spirit in beautiful language. Arguing that the Jews had an inspired book but needed more, Paul states that Christians get an inspired book plus the power of the Holy Spirit: "Now the Lord is the Spirit, and where the Spirit of the Lord is, there is freedom. And we all, who with unveiled faces contemplate the Lord's glory, are being transformed into his image with ever-increasing glory, which comes from the Lord, who is the Spirit" (2 Corinthians 3:17–18).

The Spirit works inside of us, transforming us into the image of Christ by joining with our own spirits. This is, at least in part, what is meant by the metaphor of a seal, which Paul uses a couple of times with regards to the Holy Spirit. In the Greco-Roman world, important documents were stamped with a seal that confirmed ownership and authenticity. The seal often had an image on it that reflected the name or character of the owner. Twice in the New Testament Paul says that the Holy Spirit is God's seal on believers, giving us a down payment for the life we'll enjoy after the resurrection (2 Corinthians 1:22; Ephesians 1:13). The Holy Spirit bears in us the image of God who is working to mature us spiritually.

If we were to use biological terms, we could say that the Holy Spirit is God's own DNA transplanted into our lives upon our baptism. Our physical DNA determines a great deal about our lives—what we will look like, what strengths we will possess, and how we will interact with the world. As we grow older, our DNA often makes us look more and more like one or both of our parents. For instance, the older I get, the more I look like my mother.

In the same way, our spiritual DNA is provided for us in the person of the Holy Spirit, God's image stamped on our hearts. When we faithfully obey, the Spirit responds by bringing out the Jesus in us until, one day, we mature fully into his image. In theological terminology, the Spirit "sanctifies us"—meaning the Spirit takes us after our justification and leads us to the power, the beauty, and the truthfulness of a fully spiritual life. We should never underestimate the power that comes from having God personally dwell in us through his Spirit. We are, quite literally, temples of the Spirit (1 Corinthians 6:19; 1 Corinthians 3:16). Having God dwell in us through his Spirit changes who we are; through the Spirit we literally participate in the divine nature of God (2 Peter 1:4).

This is what is meant by the phrase "filled with the Spirit." Though this term sometimes means in Scripture that a person is given some extraordinary power, it often only means that a person has become fully spiritual. For example, Barnabas is described in Acts 11:24 as "full of the Holy Spirit." Here the term seems to signify that he was a spiritually mature person.

It is in this sense that the Scriptures can actually *command* us to be filled with the Spirit (Ephesians 5:18). As we allow the Spirit to shape us into the image of Jesus, we become full of the Spirit. It is worth noting that Paul's command in Ephesians 5 to be "filled with the Spirit" is qualified by a participial phrase "*by* (or *while*) speaking to one another with psalms, hymns, and songs from the Spirit, singing and making music from your heart to the Lord always giving thanks to God . . . and submitting to one another" (Ephesians 5:19–21, AT). Singing, praising, giving thanks, and submitting to one another are a means given in this text for becoming spiritual. We fill ourselves with the Spirit when we sing, praise, give thanks, and love others.

Other phrases describe the transformational work of the Spirit in the Bible. Jesus promised to clothe the apostles with the power of the Spirit (Luke 24:49). We are taught to be led by the Spirit (Galatians 5:18). We should walk by the Spirit (Galatians 5:18). We are invited into a fellowship with the Spirit (1 Corinthians 12:13). And we can be strengthened inwardly through the power of the Spirit (Ephesians 3:16–17).

How does the Spirit sanctify us? We'll deal with this question in the next chapter, but here we must say at least one thing. The Spirit serves to draw attention to Jesus, who bears the fullness of the image of God. In Jesus' own words, the Spirit will "remind you of everything I [Jesus] have said to you"; will "testify about me"; and will "speak only what he hears" because "it is from me that he will receive what he will make known to you" (John 14:26; 15:26; 16:13–15).

DISCIPLESHIP IS FOLLOWING JESUS IN THE POWER OF THE SPIRIT.

Discipleship is following Jesus in the power of the Spirit.

We cannot become like Jesus without divine help. So God gives us a new birth in the Spirit; Christ baptizes us in the Spirit; and we are invited to be full of the Spirit. And all of this is for one overarching reason: to transform us into the image of him whom we follow.

REFLECTION & DISCUSSION QUESTIONS

1. If someone asked you to what it means to be "immersed" in God, how would you answer?

2. As a disciple of Jesus, real life is spiritual life in Christ. Before you were a disciple of Jesus, what was "real life" to you? If you are not a disciple, what do you think would change if you became a disciple?

3. Read Acts 4:31. How did the Holy Spirit transform the lives of Peter and John?

4. Paul uses the metaphor of a "seal" in Ephesians 1:13–14 to describe the Holy Spirit, a picture of the Spirit's ownership and authority. How does this description change your view of the Holy Spirit and his role in your life?

5. According to the Scripture mentioned in this chapter, what does it mean to be "filled with the Spirit"?

6. The phrases "clothed in the Spirit," "led by," "walking in," "fellowship with," and being "strengthened inwardly by" are all descriptions of the transformational work of the Spirit. Which of these do you long for in your life the most and why?

4

HOW DOES THE HOLY SPIRIT MAKE US LIKE JESUS?

Answer: The Holy Spirit makes us like Jesus by uniting us with other believers, by interceding with the Father on our behalf, by producing the goodness of Jesus in our lives, and by equipping us for the mission of Jesus.

But the fruit of the Spirit is love, joy, peace, forbearance, kindness, goodness, faithfulness, gentleness and self-control. Against such things there is no law.
— Galatians 5:22–23

So the Holy Spirit transforms us into the image of Jesus. This is *his work*, not ours. But how does he work? Can we say exactly what the Spirit does to transform us into Christ's image? A full answer to this question would require volumes of material, but for our purposes, I'll summarize the methods of the Spirit's work under four headings. Each heading is a biblical category from which we'll draw out implications for how the Spirit transforms our lives.

THE SPIRIT UNITES US WITH OTHER BELIEVERS

First, we should note that following Jesus is not a solitary endeavor. When we become a believer, we join a worldwide communion of believers, and our relationship with them is critical to our becoming like Jesus. Just as God lives in the communion of a Holy Trinity, so we live in a holy communion—of the church.

Not only are our individual bodies temples of the Spirit; the collective body of the church is a temple of the Holy Spirit (1 Corinthians 3:16–17). We are united to one another through the same Spirit (1 Corinthians 12:13), and it is through the church that we unite to serve as priests to the world, offering up to God our sacrifice, worship, praise, and intercession. We are united together through him. It's worth noting that

1 Corinthians and Ephesians—two books that mention the Spirit as much as any in the Bible—mention him often in connection with the unity and fellowship of the community of believers.

Nothing compares to the beauty of a united fellowship whose members know that they all share in the same Spirit. We love each other in the same Spirit (Philippians 2:2); we unite with one another through the power of the Spirit (Ephesians 4:3); and we refuse to divide with one another because of the work of the Spirit (1 Corinthians 3:16ff). In fact, every "one another" command in the New Testament is possible for the believer only because we are bound together by the Spirit.

The result? The unity of the Spirit in the church allows us to present ourselves to the world as the mature body of Christ, unwavering in our faith (Ephesians 4:9–16).

THE SPIRIT INTERCEDES WITH THE FATHER ON OUR BEHALF

The Holy Spirit also intercedes with the Father on our behalf. Jesus had promised that he would give the apostles the Holy Spirit, whom he called "the Counselor"—a term that could well be translated as "the Attorney" (John 14:16, AT). By using this term, Jesus envisioned the Spirit working as an intermediary. Paul goes further on this, explaining that "he who searches our hearts knows the mind of the Spirit, because the Spirit intercedes for God's people in accordance with the will of God" (Romans 8:27). Throughout Romans 8 Paul indicates how the Spirit does this: he sets us free from the bondage of our broken will, which chains us to our sin. He does this by dwelling within us, replacing our broken will by the power of God. And this power breaks our chains. The more we are filled with the Spirit, the less we want to sin, and the freer we become. The Spirit sets us free, and in that sense, he can be said to intercede for us.

Perhaps another way to envision the intercessory work of the Spirit is to imagine him witnessing to the Father about our struggles, our efforts, our fruit, and our mission—all of which he can do because he lives within us and knows us well. In any case, the intercessory work of the Spirit is what enables us to cry out "Abba" to God in our time of need (Romans 8:15).

He joins us to God just as our physical DNA joins us to our parents. He presents our case to God. When we struggle, suffer, experience despair, or face loneliness, the Holy Spirit appeals to the Father on our behalf. He offers us a pathway to God's healing grace.

THE SPIRIT PRODUCES THE GOODNESS OF JESUS IN OUR LIVES

In Galatians 5, Paul contrasts the works of the flesh with the virtues of the Spirit. "But the fruit of the Spirit is love, joy, peace, forbearance, kindness, goodness, faithfulness, gentleness and self-control" (Galatians 5:22–23). Having the Spirit's fruit in our lives, he explains, is to "live by the Spirit" and "keep in step with the Spirit" (v. 25). The Spirit makes us like Jesus by producing the goodness of Jesus in our lives.

It is important to note Paul's use of the term "fruit" in this text. Paul does not call the nine virtues of Galatians 5 "works," even though we must put forth effort to attain them. Rather, he terms these virtues "fruit." "Fruit" suggests that these moral traits will naturally flow out of those who live in the Spirit. In other words, if we permit the Spirit to have his way in our lives, a virtuous, Christlike life will emerge. Even though they must be cultivated, apple trees don't have to work at producing apples—it is in their DNA. And though Christian virtues must be cultivated in the life of the believer, Spirit-filled people naturally produce the virtues of Christ. It's in their DNA.

SPIRIT-FILLED PEOPLE NATURALLY PRODUCE THE VIRTUES OF CHRIST.

Indeed, without the Spirit, we simply cannot produce the fruit of a Jesus-styled life, for without the Spirit we are forever stuck in the weakness of the flesh. We face a spiritual battle, and flesh alone cannot defeat the spiritual forces of evil (Ephesians 6:12). Victory requires the power of God's Spirit. Jesus is said to have cast out evil spirits through the power of God's Holy Spirit (Matthew 12:28). In the same way, to overcome the sinful desires of the body, we need the power of the Spirit of God.

At this point, it is important to note several texts that give us a warning about the work of the Spirit: Ephesians 4:30, which warns us not to grieve the Spirit; 1 Thessalonians 5:19, which teaches us not to put out the Spirit's fire; and Mark 3:28–30, where Jesus warns us about speaking against the Holy Spirit.[11] These warnings reveal an important truth: we cannot *force* the Spirit to work in us, no more than one can force an apple tree to produce apples. But we can *hinder* the work of the Spirit, just as we can hinder the growth of apples through neglecting the tree. We are taught to seek God according to the Spirit, so that we will set our minds on what the Spirit desires (Romans 8: 5–6). If we do not pursue God this way but live by our flesh, we will thwart the work of the Spirit and hinder the fruit he wants to produce in us. This is why we have an obligation to put to death the misdeeds of the body so that the Spirit can produce the fruit of rightness in our lives (Romans 8:12–13). We are encouraged to keep alive our "spiritual fervor" (Romans 12:11). The Spirit does not override our free will, as 1 Corinthians 14 makes clear (see, for example, 14:32). Rather, the Spirit acts in concert with our will, empowering us to choose that which is holy, while leaving us free to choose—at our peril—to be unholy.

If we cultivate the Spirit in our lives, he will produce in us the goodness of Jesus—from one degree of glory to another.

THE SPIRIT EQUIPS US FOR THE MISSION OF JESUS

In addition to joining us to the people of God, interceding for us, and producing fruit in our lives, the Holy Spirit distributes gifts to equip us for the mission of Jesus. In the Old Testament, the Spirit equipped certain people to perform the tasks to which God had called them. He gave Samson his strength (Judges 15:14); he supplied the seventy elders with their judicial abilities (Numbers 11:17); he gave David leadership powers (1 Samuel 16:13); and he even gave technical skill to Bezalel, who made designs for the tabernacle (Exodus 31:2–3).

Three passages in the New Testament list the main spiritual gifts the Spirit gives to Christians: Romans 12, 1 Corinthians 12, and Ephesians 4. In these texts, the gifts sometimes appear to describe a limited office of some sort. At other times, however, these gifts appear to be general in nature—referring to any power, talent, or opportunity given by God for the purpose of fulfilling the mission of Jesus.

Before we look at some specific gifts, it is important we remember that all the gifts are given for the purpose of building up the body. They are not given for personal gratification: "Now to each one the manifestation of the Spirit is given for the common good" (1 Corinthians 12:7). This point matters greatly because we might be tempted to seek the gifts for our own gratification, but that's not why the Spirit gives his gifts. He gives them so we can carry out the mission of Jesus (Romans 12:4ff; Ephesians 4:12ff).

So what about the gifts? The more general gifts of the Spirit include such things as generosity, encouragement, leadership, discernment, and the like. It is fairly obvious how these gifts can be used to build up the body of Christ. If you have the gift of generosity, you should actively seek ways to fund good works for Jesus. If you have the gift of leadership, you should offer it to help others mature in faith. If you are an encourager, you should seek ways to lift up others. If you are a teacher, you should help others come to know the truth of Christ.

In addition to what appear to be these more ordinary gifts, however, there are other gifts mentioned in the New Testament that seem specialized—even comparable to an office. Let's take a brief look at three of these.

Apostleship. Though occasionally the Greek term for "apostle" may mean "missionary" in the Bible (e.g., Romans 16:7), there is a specialized use of the term "apostle" that refers to the twelve inspired disciples called during the earthly ministry of Jesus (as well as their designated successors—Matthias and Paul). The apostles were endowed with the authority to reveal the Word on behalf of Jesus (Matthew 16:16–18; John 14–16). They were expected to have been with Jesus personally (Acts 1:21–22). They demonstrated their authority as apostles through their ability to perform signs, wonders, and powers (2 Corinthians 12:12; Hebrews 2:2–4). Apostles were chosen directly by the Lord (see Mark 3:13–19; Galatians 1:1). They were given the keys to the kingdom of God (Matthew 16:16–19). They had the ability to confer gifts on others (Acts 8:17–18). The apostles have a unique place in heaven: their names are inscribed forever in the foundations of heaven's wall (Revelation 21:14). Peter says that we are to embrace the command of the Lord as it was given through the apostles (2 Peter 3:2). Believers today participate in the work of the apostles when we accept their writings, the Scriptures. Though we still have "missionaries" in the contemporary church, we should not claim the title "apostle" today—at least not in the sense of the Twelve—since the office of the apostle was restricted to the Twelve plus Paul and perhaps a few others, and these were not replaced in subsequent generations with others who held their unique status.[12]

Prophet. In the Old Testament, the gift of prophecy was given to ensure that the people of God received the reliable and infallible Word of God. It appears that the New Testament may sometimes use the term "prophet" in a more general way—simply as one who proclaims the Word of God based on the works of the inspired authors of Scripture.[13] This seems to be the case in 1 Corinthians 14, where it seems that a number of church members were taking turns "prophesying." In a stricter sense, however, the default New Testament use of "prophet" meant someone who held a similar office as did an "apostle," and the gift of prophecy was limited primarily to those who worked alongside the apostles. This is why Ephesians 2:18–19 says that the church is built upon the foundation of the apostles and prophets. It also explains why Peter can affirm that the writings of the prophets did not have their origins in the minds of the prophets, but were delivered by the Spirit himself (2 Peter 1:20–21). The work of these prophets is preserved for us in the Scriptures, alongside the work of the apostles.

As we think of prophecy, we should be mindful that the Bible repeatedly warns against false prophets and false prophecies, as it also warns against false apostles.[14] Not everyone who claims to be speaking the very words of God should be believed. Rather, we are to test people's claims against the truth of Scripture. Those who fabricate utterances in the name of God are guilty of a serious sin.

Miracle worker and healer. Paul does not define these gifts when he mentions them in 1 Corinthians 12, but they seem to mean someone who can perform, by the power of the Spirit, powerful deeds such as healing the sick. The New Testament rarely gives examples of anyone working miracles or healing others except for Jesus and the apostles, so we should not assume that receiving the Spirit automatically gives us the ability to perform these powers. After all, none other than John the Baptist was filled with the Spirit, but he never performed a miracle (Luke 1:15; John 10:41). Whether or not we can receive the gift of powers today, we must, however, always gratefully accept that *God* still performs powers. Healings still occur, regardless of whether or not the Spirit gives *us* that particular gift.

Speaking in tongues. In addition to these three "offices," the Bible also mentions the phenomenon of tongue-speaking. What is tongue-speaking? The question has been much debated in Christian history, especially in the last one hundred years. We should note that the subject is only occasionally mentioned in the Bible; only a handful of texts bring it up (Mark 16:17; Acts 2; 19:6; and 1 Corinthians 12–14). In technical language, the phenomenon is called "glossolalia" in English, which is a combination of the Greek terms for "tongues" and "speaking." There appear to be two kinds of glossolalia in the New Testament, although the New Testament doesn't distinguish these. The first is when a speaker appears to speak in a real human language that the speaker doesn't actually know. We might call this "xenolalia" (although the term is not used in the New Testament). Xenolalia appears to be what happened in Acts 2, where the early church preached in numerous languages that are even called "dialects" by Luke (Acts 2:8, AT). The second use of "tongues" appears to be private utterances—not words of an actual human language. We might call this "idiolalia" (although, again, the term is not used in the New Testament). Idiolalia can range from private groans all the way to the rhythmic utterance of syllables using tones and inflections and sounding a lot like a real human language.

Xenolalia is likely rare based on its rarity in the New Testament, although we have examples of missionaries using this gift, even in the twenty-first century.

If idiolalia includes "groaning with words we cannot utter," as mentioned in Romans 8:26 (AT), the phenomenon appears to be widespread among believers. Who hasn't groaned in times of distress with sighs and moans that are not actual language? If by "idiolalia" we mean the full expression of syllables spoken like a real language (although not any known language), the phenomenon is generally practiced only by those who identify as charismatics.[15] In either case, such idiolalia shouldn't pretend to be authoritative, as though it possesses apostolic or prophetic authority. Rather, it is simply the soul bypassing ordinary language in response to the ups and downs of the Christian life—not unlike humming, self-talk, or even a person singing unaware. It is like the soothing baby talk a child uses to calm themselves down.[16]

We should note that Paul limits the use of *tongues*: it should not be done in a congregational gathering unless it can be interpreted (1 Corinthians 14:19, 26, 28), and it should be used in public only if it builds up the body of believers.

What are we to make of the gifts of prophecy, healing, and tongues today? Though claims to these gifts are very common in today's global church, for centuries such claims were rare. In fact, for most of the history of the church, the foundation of the Scriptures, the service of the pastor, and the teaching ministry of the church were understood to have made prophecy, healing, and tongues unnecessary. But perspectives changed in the opening years of the 1900s, when the Pentecostal movement broke out in America. Though Pentecostalism started with only a few thousand members, various charismatic practices born out of Pentecostalism are now embraced by as many as half of the world's Christians.[17]

The leaders at the Renew.org Network have different understandings on specifics with regard to the gifts of the Spirit, even though all our leaders agree to seek all that God has for us through his Spirit. The Renew.org Network is a movement that relies on God's Spirit, especially through the classic spiritual habits of regular fasting and prayer. Some of our leaders do not see God fully activating the special gifts of tongues, prophecy, or healing today, while others do witness and uphold those activations.

I personally believe that, rightly understood, God still gives these gifts. God still gives some the ability to speak truth to current circumstances (prophecy). He still gives some a special calling to pray for healing, prayers to which he often says yes (healing). And he still gives, on occasion, xenolalia, and, much more commonly, idiolalia (tongue-speaking).

Even so, I do not believe these gifts are inspired in the same way as were the prophets and apostles of the Bible. Indeed, no gift we might receive today should be viewed as possessing the same authority as Scripture.

Scripture was written under the unique inspiration of the apostles, and so Scripture possesses final authority. Scripture is infallible. We are not apostles, nor do we live in the apostolic age. So none of our gifts should claim such inspiration, infallibility, or apostolic authority. Rather, our gifts are designed to encourage us to go back to the authority of the inspired and infallible Bible. Nothing can stand in the place of the Scriptures.

SCRIPTURE POSSESSES FINAL AUTHORITY. SCRIPTURE IS INFALLIBLE.

Further, we should exercise caution with respect to these spiritual gifts. Not every claim of prophecy, healing, and tongues represents authentic works of the Holy Spirit. There are well-documented examples of frauds who have claimed to possess such gifts—one only need think of the myriad of television evangelists whose deceit has been exposed. Such individuals and their thousands of supporters are an embarrassment to the church. They insult the Spirit. Further, some prominent charismatic leaders have been associated with heretical teachings—such as denying the deity of Christ or preaching the health-and-wealth gospel. The association of claims of prophecy and tongues with such heresies is a caution against accepting every claim to such gifts. The church should not discourage the gifts of God when rightly understood. But the church also should not accept every claim that is made. Discernment and wisdom should guide us in exercising the gifts the Spirit gives.

Those who seek the empowerment and use of these special gifts in a public manner should seek to use them in step with the leadership of their local church and with what is fitting and orderly (1 Corinthians 14:40).

To conclude, then, the Spirit distributes gifts for the building up of the body, and in this way, he helps transform us into the image of Jesus. While we can describe the ways the Spirit does this, we should not be surprised that his gifting will remain something of a mystery. As Jesus says, the Spirit moves like the wind—we see its effects, but cannot really tell how it works (John 3:8). Regardless of how the Spirit does it, because we have him in our lives, we can become like our Lord. So we should seek the gifts of the Lord, and in so doing, we can experience his power in our lives (1 Corinthians 14:1).

REFLECTION & DISCUSSION QUESTIONS

1. What community of believers are you a part of that encourages you in the ways of Jesus? How does the Holy Spirit bring unity to the group, even when there are differences?

2. How would you describe to a new believer what it means that the Holy Spirit intercedes for us?

3. Contrast Galatians 5:19–21 with Galatians 5:22–23. Is it possible to have the fruit of the Spirit without allowing the Holy Spirit to reign over your life? Why?

4. Read Ephesians 4:30. In what ways have you grieved or put out the fire of the Spirit in your life?

5. The gifts that the Holy Spirit gives are to be used for the purposes of fulfilling the mission of Jesus. For example, Romans 12 lists gifts such as teaching, serving, encouraging, and showing mercy. How have you used your gifts to fulfill the mission of Jesus?

6. This chapter describes several ways that the Holy Spirit makes us more like Jesus. Which of these ways will you ask God to use in your life?

5

HOW DO WE SEEK THE HOLY SPIRIT'S LEADERSHIP IN OUR LIVES?

Answer: We open our lives to the Holy Spirit's leadership with spiritual practices such as prayer, fasting, and virtuous living.

And pray in the Spirit on all occasions with all kinds of prayers and requests. With this in mind, be alert and always keep on praying for all the Lord's people.
— Ephesians 6:18

Several Scripture passages mention being "led by the Spirit":

- "Teach me to do your will, for you are my God; may your good Spirit lead me on level ground" (Psalm 143:10).
- "Then Jesus was led by the Spirit into the wilderness to be tempted by the devil" (Matthew 4:1).
- "For those who are led by the Spirit of God are the children of God" (Romans 8:14).
- "He carried me away in the Spirit to a mountain great and high, and showed me the Holy City, Jerusalem, coming down out of heaven from God" (Revelation 21:10).

Though the term "led by the Spirit" sometimes appears simply to mean that a person is in deep communion with God, at other times the term appears to be closely connected to prayer, fasting, and even the feeling of being compelled to do something virtuous (e.g., Ezekiel 37:1; Mark 1:12; Acts 8:29; 15:28; 16:6–7; 20:22; Revelation 4:2). In light of these Scripture passages, how are we led by the Spirit today?

I have already stated that we cannot control or manipulate the Spirit. We can only submit to the divine work that he wants to do. But this does not mean that there is nothing we should do. On the contrary, in addition to repenting of our sin and focusing our life on Jesus, we must ask the Spirit to have his way in our lives. This is of critical importance. If we do not ask, we will not receive.

WE MUST ASK THE SPIRIT TO HAVE HIS WAY IN OUR LIVES.

So, at the simplest level, we are led by the Spirit when we ask God to show us the spiritual dimension of our lives and live out his response. For example, when struggling in your marriage, being led by the Spirit can mean looking at your struggle not as between flesh and blood, but between the Holy Spirit *in us* and the powers of evil working *against us*. It involves perceiving the lies the evil one uses to make you bitter, rageful, unfaithful, and the like. It involves asking the Spirit to use your struggles to create in you love, righteousness, faith, hope, and the like (Ephesians 6:10ff).

Consider how this is like running a race. I've run numerous charity races in my life, and at every one of them I've seen encouragers standing on the side of the road. They supply water, shout out encouragement, and remind me of how little distance I have to go. The race depends on my legs and lungs. But the commentary on the race is offered by the encouragers, who help me remember why I chose such a painful activity. In the same way, whenever we seek to live a godlike life, there are spiritual forces of evil shouting out lies to us: "You cannot do this," "It's not worth it," "You should cheat," and the like. But there is also the Holy Spirit cheering us on: "This will save lives," "You are doing the right thing," "You will finish strong." Being led by the Spirit involves refusing to listen to the lies of the evil one. Instead, we listen to the voice of the Spirit.

This is, at least in part, what it means to say that the Spirit tugs at our consciences, opens the eyes of our hearts, and gives us spiritual aspirations. This is promised in Acts 2, when Peter preached that the last days—in which we currently find ourselves—will be marked by dreams and visions from the Spirit. Peter concluded his sermon by saying that this same Spirit was available to anyone who repented and was baptized—"for all whom the Lord our God will call" (Acts 2:17–18, 38–39).

And as in biblical examples, being led by the Spirit today is closely connected to prayer and fasting. Indeed, it may be that the Spirit holds the deepest levels of guidance *only* for those who are fully devoted to prayer and fasting. And so we see a connection between prayer and the Holy Spirit in the Scriptures. Paul commands us to "pray in the Spirit" on all occasions, and he connects this with spiritual alertness (Ephesians 6:18–19). Jude says something similar, connecting prayer in the Spirit with actively waiting for the coming Jesus (Jude 20–21). Jesus said that the Father will give the Holy Spirit to those who ask (Luke 11:13).

So in order to be led by the Spirit, we must learn the disciplines, especially those focused on prayer and fasting. This makes sense for through intense prayer and fasting we empty ourselves of fleshly desires and worldly interests and become increasingly dependent on the power of God. It's worth remembering that the outpouring of the Holy Spirit in Acts 2:19—described with such awe-inspiring terms as "blood, fire, and billows of smoke"—came only after the church had constantly devoted itself to prayer in Acts 1:14. If we want Acts 2 results, we must practice Acts 1 prayer.

In fact, it's possible that one reason why many of us rarely experience signs, wonders, and powers in our lives is that we don't seriously pray, fast, or take great risks of faith for Christ. Powerful experiences are regular occurrences for those who take great risks, who fast intensely, who pray day and night—for those who are so deeply immersed in the Spirit that they become wholly unconcerned with what the world might think. If you live a spiritually boring life, you will get spiritually boring results. But when you stick out your neck for Christ, seasoned by prayer and fasting, you will see more and more signs, wonders, and powers.

IF YOU LIVE A SPIRITUALLY BORING LIFE, YOU WILL GET SPIRITUALLY BORING RESULTS.

It just grows more for those who are increasingly led by the Spirit of God.

The Holy Spirit will not force you to follow his lead, and the world with its secular veil will make following the Spirit difficult. But if you want to be led by the Spirit and thereby experience the richness of life that God has intended for you, devote yourself to prayer and fasting. There the Spirit opens the eyes of our hearts and draws us to him. Devote yourself to prayer and fasting, and the Spirit will respond in one way or another. You will see him, and he will lead you where he wants you to go. You will experience the power, the fruit, and the transformation the Spirit provides.

There is a spiritual dimension to everything we do. Look for it, and live in that dimension. Refuse to follow the fleshly side of life. Follow the spiritual life instead.

REFLECTION & DISCUSSION QUESTIONS

1. Describe a time in your life when you felt truly led by the Spirit.

2. Give an example of a situation that, if you completely turn it over to the Spirit, then you will have a different perspective on the outcome of the situation.

3. What lies do you sometimes believe? What would your "encourager," the Holy Spirit, say instead to replace those lies?

4. Is your prayer life as active as you want it to be? If not, is it an issue of your heart, or is it life logistics? What practical steps can you take to change?

5. If you have not regularly practiced fasting, what is stopping you from participating in this spiritual discipline?

6. Think of someone in your life who seems particularly led by the Spirit. What sets them apart in your mind? What are practical ways you can be like them and develop more of the Holy Spirit in your life?

CONCLUSION

The Holy Spirit is essential to the life of the believer. In fact, it is not possible to be a follower of Jesus without the Spirit of God: "If anyone does not have the Spirit of Christ, they do not belong to Christ" (Romans 8:9). But with the Holy Spirit in our lives, we celebrate our status as God's children (Romans 8:14–15) who receive the love of God poured into our hearts (Romans 5:5), liberating us from the bondage of sin and death (Romans 8:2–4), giving us life and peace (Romans 8:6), including us in Christ (Romans 8:9), sanctifying us (Romans 15:16), washing us (1 Corinthians 6:11), transforming us (2 Corinthians 3:17–18), producing fruit in us (Galatians 5:22–23), and giving us access to the Father (Ephesians 2:18).

With the Holy Spirit, we discover who God is, and we are empowered to become like him. Thank God for his Spirit!

I once read an imaginative story about a man who had a dream in which he visited heaven's mansion. While there, he was taken by the Lord into heaven's library, where he began to browse the amazing collection. Soon, he found a volume on a shelf that contained the complete biography of the man's life. Thrilled, he opened the book and read of all sorts of amazing things that the Spirit had accomplished in his life—people he had brought to the Lord, amazing powers and wonders he had experienced, boundless fruit God had developed in his life, a profound sense of peace and joy that permeated everything he did, and a whole lot more.

Looking at the Lord, he said, "Lord, this is a fantastic biography of my life, but there's a problem. I never experienced any of this. It's not accurate!" The Lord responded by reaching for a flimsy manila folder that had only a page or two of handwritten notes in it. "You're right," the Lord responded. Then, handing the manila folder to the man, the Lord explained: "This folder is your *actual* biography. The amazing biography in the big book is the life I wanted to give you. It's what you would have had if you had asked for my Spirit!"

The Holy Spirit is here! May God give us the insight and courage to ask for him—and act in faithful obedience to receive the life God wants to give us by his Spirit.

APPENDIX A

BOOK RECOMMENDATIONS FOR FURTHER STUDY

Leonard Allen, *Poured Out: The Spirit of God Empowering the Mission of God* (Abilene: ACU Press, 2018).

Francis Chan, *Forgotten God: Reversing Our Tragic Neglect of the Holy Spirit* (Colorado Springs: David C. Cook, 2009).

Gordon Fee, *God's Empowering Presence: The Holy Spirit in the Letters of Paul* (Peabody: Hendrickson Publishers, 1994).

Michael Green, *I Believe in the Holy Spirit* (Grand Rapids: Eerdmans, 1975).

David Roadcup, Michael Eagle, et al., *Prayer and Fasting: Moving with the Spirit to Renew Our Minds, Bodies, and Churches* (Renew.org, 2020).

M. James Sawyer and Daniel B. Wallace, eds., *Who's Afraid of the Holy Spirit?* (Dallas: Biblical Studies Press, 2005).

APPENDIX B

RENEW.ORG NETWORK LEADERS' VALUES AND FAITH STATEMENTS

Mission: We Renew the Teachings of Jesus to Fuel Disciple Making

---

Vision: A collaborative network equipping millions of disciples, disciple makers, and church planters among all ethnicities.

SEVEN VALUES

Renewal in the Bible and in history follows a discernible outline that can be summarized by seven key elements. We champion these elements as our core values. They are listed in a sequential pattern that is typical of renewal, and it all starts with God.

1. *Renewing by God's Spirit.* We believe that God is the author of renewal and that he invites us to access and join him through prayer and fasting for the Holy Spirit's work of renewal.
2. *Following God's Word.* We learn the ways of God with lasting clarity and conviction by trusting God's Word and what it teaches as the objective foundation for renewal and life.
3. *Surrendering to Jesus' Lordship.* The gospel teaches us that Jesus is Messiah (King) and Lord. He calls everyone to salvation (in eternity) and discipleship (in this life) through a faith commitment that is expressed in repentance, confession, and baptism. Repentance and surrender to Jesus as Lord is the never-ending cycle for life in Jesus' kingdom, and it is empowered by the Spirit.
4. *Championing disciple making.* Jesus personally gave us his model of disciple making, which he demonstrated with his disciples. Those same principles from the life of Jesus should be utilized as we make disciples today and champion discipleship as the core mission of the local church.
5. *Loving like Jesus.* Jesus showed us the true meaning of love and taught us that sacrificial love is the

distinguishing character trait of true disciples (and true renewal). Sacrificial love is the foundation for our relationships both in the church and in the world.

6. *Living in holiness.* Just as Jesus lived differently from the world, the people in his church will learn to live differently than the world. Even when it is difficult, we show that God's kingdom is an alternative kingdom to the world.
7. *Leading courageously.* God always uses leaders in renewal who live by a prayerful, risk-taking faith. Renewal will be led by bold and courageous leaders—who make disciples, plant churches, and create disciple making movements.

TEN FAITH STATEMENTS

We believe that Jesus Christ is Lord. We are a group of church leaders inviting others to join the theological and disciple making journey described below. We want to trust and follow Jesus Christ to the glory of God the Father in the power of the Holy Spirit. We are committed to *restoring* the kingdom vision of Jesus and the apostles, especially the *message* of Jesus' gospel, the *method* of disciple making he showed us, and the *model* of what a community of his disciples, at their best, can become.

We live in a time when cultural pressures are forcing us to face numerous difficulties and complexities in following God. Many are losing their resolve. We trust that God is gracious and forgives the errors of those with genuine faith in his Son, but our desire is to be faithful in all things.

Our focus is disciple making, which is both reaching lost people (evangelism) and bringing people to maturity (sanctification). We seek to be a movement of disciple making leaders who make disciples and other disciple makers. We want to renew existing churches and help plant multiplying churches.

1. *God's Word.* We believe God gave us the sixty-six books of the Bible to be received as the inspired, authoritative, and infallible Word of God for salvation and life. The documents of Scripture come to us as diverse literary and historical writings. Despite their complexities, they can be understood, trusted, and followed. We want to do the hard work of wrestling to understand Scripture in order to obey God. We want to avoid the errors of interpreting Scripture through the sentimental lens of our feelings and opinions or through a complex re-interpretation of plain meanings so that the Bible says what our culture says. Ours is a time for both clear thinking and courage. Because the Holy Spirit inspired all sixty-six books, we honor Jesus' Lordship by submitting our lives to all that God has for us in them.

Psalm 1; 119; Deuteronomy 4:1–6; 6:1–9; 2 Chronicles 34; Nehemiah 8; Matthew 5:1–7:28; 15:6–9; John 12:44–50; Matthew 28:19; Acts 2:42; 17:10–11; 2 Timothy 3:16–4:4; 1 Peter 1:20–21.

2. *Christian convictions.* We believe the Scriptures reveal three distinct elements of the faith: *essential* elements which are necessary for salvation; *important* elements which are to be pursued so that we faithfully follow Christ; and *personal* elements or opinion. The gospel is *essential.* Every person who is indwelt and sealed by God's Holy Spirit because of their faith in the gospel is a brother or a sister in Christ. *Important* but secondary elements of the faith are vital. Our faithfulness to God requires us to seek and pursue them, even as we acknowledge that our salvation may not be dependent on getting them right. And thirdly, there are personal matters of opinion, disputable areas where God gives us personal freedom. But we are never at liberty to express our freedom in a way that causes others to stumble in sin. In all things, we want to show understanding, kindness, and love.

1 Corinthians 15:1–8; Romans 1:15–17; Galatians 1:6–9; 2 Timothy 2:8; Ephesians 1:13–14; 4:4–6; Romans 8:9; 1 Corinthians 12:13; 1 Timothy 4:16; 2 Timothy 3:16–4:4;

Matthew 15:6–9; Acts 20:32; 1 Corinthians 11:1–2; 1 John 2:3–4; 2 Peter 3:14–16; Romans 14:1–23.

3. *The gospel.* We believe God created all things and made human beings in his image, so that we could enjoy a relationship with him and each other. But we lost our way, through Satan's influence. We are now spiritually dead, separated from God. Without his help, we gravitate toward sin and self-rule. The gospel is God's good news of reconciliation. It was promised to Abraham and David and revealed in Jesus' life, ministry, teaching, and sacrificial death on the cross. The gospel is the saving action of the triune God. The Father sent the Son into the world to take on human flesh and redeem us. Jesus came as the promised Messiah of the Old Testament. He ushered in the kingdom of God, died for our sins according to Scripture, was buried, and was raised on the third day. He defeated sin and death and ascended to heaven. He is seated at the right hand of God as Lord and he is coming back for his disciples. Through the Spirit, we are transformed and sanctified. God will raise everyone for the final judgment. Those who trusted and followed Jesus by faith will not experience punishment for their sins and separation from God in hell. Instead, we will join together with God in the renewal of all things in the consummated kingdom. We will live

together in the new heaven and new earth where we will glorify God and enjoy him forever.

Genesis 1–3; Romans 3:10–12; 7:8–25;
Genesis 12:1–3; Galatians 3:6–9; Isaiah 11:1–4;
2 Samuel 7:1–16; Micah 5:2–4; Daniel 2:44–45;
Luke 1:33; John 1:1–3; Matthew 4:17;
1 Corinthians 15:1–8; Acts 1:11; 2:36; 3:19–21;
Colossians 3:1; Matthew 25:31–32; Revelation 21:1ff;
Romans 3:21–26.

4. *Faithful faith.* We believe that people are saved by grace through faith. The gospel of Jesus' kingdom calls people to both salvation and discipleship—no exceptions, no excuses. Faith is more than mere intellectual agreement or emotional warmth toward God. It is living and active; faith is surrendering our self-rule to the rule of God through Jesus in the power of the Spirit. We surrender by trusting and following Jesus as both Savior and Lord in all things. Faith includes allegiance, loyalty, and faithfulness to him.

Ephesians 2:8–9; Mark 8:34–38; Luke 14:25–35;
Romans 1:3, 5; 16:25–26; Galatians 2:20;
James 2:14–26; Matthew 7:21–23; Galatians 4:19;
Matthew 28:19–20; 2 Corinthians 3:3, 17–18;
Colossians 1:28.

5. *New birth.* God so loved the world that he gave his one and only Son, that whoever believes in him shall not perish but have eternal life. To believe in Jesus means we trust and follow him as both Savior and Lord. When we commit to trust and follow Jesus, we express this faith by repenting from sin, confessing his name, and receiving baptism by immersion in water. Baptism, as an expression of faith, is for the remission of sins. We uphold baptism as the normative means of entry into the life of discipleship. It marks our commitment to regularly die to ourselves and rise to live for Christ in the power of the Holy Spirit. We believe God sovereignly saves as he sees fit, but we are bound by Scripture to uphold this teaching about surrendering to Jesus in faith through repentance, confession, and baptism.

1 Corinthians 8:6; John 3:1–9; 3:16–18; 3:19–21; Luke 13:3–5; 24:46–47; Acts 2:38; 3:19; 8:36–38; 16:31–33; 17:30; 20:21; 22:16; 26:20; Galatians 3:26–27; Romans 6:1–4; 10:9–10; 1 Peter 3:21; Romans 2:25–29; 2 Chronicles 30:17–19; Matthew 28:19–20; Galatians 2:20; Acts 18:24–26.

6. *Holy Spirit.* We believe God's desire is for everyone to be saved and come to the knowledge of the truth. Many hear the gospel but do not believe it because they

are blinded by Satan and resist the pull of the Holy Spirit. We encourage everyone to listen to the Word and let the Holy Spirit convict them of their sin and draw them into a relationship with God through Jesus. We believe that when we are born again and indwelt by the Holy Spirit, we are to live as people who are filled, empowered, and led by the Holy Spirit. This is how we walk with God and discern his voice. A prayerful life, rich in the Holy Spirit, is fundamental to true discipleship and living in step with the kingdom reign of Jesus. We seek to be a prayerful, Spirit-led fellowship.

1 Timothy 2:4; John 16:7–11; Acts 7:51; 1 John 2:20, 27; John 3:5; Ephesians 1:13–14; 5:18; Galatians 5:16–25; Romans 8:5–11; Acts 1:14; 2:42; 6:6; 9:40; 12:5; 13:3; 14:23; 20:36; 2 Corinthians 3:3.

7. *Disciple making.* We believe the core mission of the local church is making disciples of Jesus Christ—it is God's plan "A" to redeem the world and manifest the reign of his kingdom. We want to be disciples who make disciples because of our love for God and others. We personally seek to become more and more like Jesus through his Spirit so that Jesus would live through us. To help us focus on Jesus, his sacrifice on the cross, our unity in him, and his coming return, we typically share

communion in our weekly gatherings. We desire the fruits of biblical disciple making which are disciples who live and love like Jesus and "go" into every corner of society and to the ends of the earth. Disciple making is the engine that drives our missional service to those outside the church. We seek to be known where we live for the good that we do in our communities. We love and serve all people, as Jesus did, no strings attached. At the same time, as we do good for others, we also seek to form relational bridges that we prayerfully hope will open doors for teaching people the gospel of the kingdom and the way of salvation.

Matthew 28:19–20; Galatians 4:19;
Acts 2:41; Philippians 1:20–21; Colossians 1:27–29;
2 Corinthians 3:3; 1 Thessalonians 2:19–20;
John 13:34–35; 1 John 3:16; 1 Corinthians 13:1–13;
Luke 22:14–23; 1 Corinthians 11:17–24; Acts 20:7.

8. *Kingdom life.* We believe in the present kingdom reign of God, the power of the Holy Spirit to transform people, and the priority of the local church. God's holiness should lead our churches to reject lifestyles characterized by pride, sexual immorality, homosexuality, easy divorce, idolatry, greed, materialism, gossip, slander, racism, violence, and the like. God's love should lead our churches to emphasize love as the distinguishing sign of

a true disciple. Love for one another should make the church like an extended family—a fellowship of married people, singles, elderly, and children who are all brothers and sisters to one another. The love of the extended church family to one another is vitally important. Love should be expressed in both service to the church and to the surrounding community. It leads to the breaking down of walls (racial, social, political), evangelism, acts of mercy, compassion, forgiveness, and the like. By demonstrating the ways of Jesus, the church reveals God's kingdom reign to the watching world.

1 Corinthians 1:2; Galatians 5:19–21;
Ephesians 5:3–7; Colossians 3:5–9;
Matthew 19:3–12; Romans 1:26–32; 14:17–18;
1 Peter 1:15–16; Matthew 25:31–46;
John 13:34–35; Colossians 3:12–13; 1 John 3:16;
1 Corinthians 13:1–13; 2 Corinthians 5:16–21.

9. *Counter-cultural living.* We believe Jesus' Lordship through Scripture will lead us to be a distinct light in the world. We follow the first and second Great Commandments where love and loyalty to God come first and love for others comes second. So we prioritize the gospel and one's relationship with God, with a strong commitment to love people in their secondary points of need too. The gospel is God's light for us. It teaches us

grace, mercy, and love. It also teaches us God's holiness, justice, and the reality of hell which led to Jesus' sacrifice of atonement for us. God's light is grace and truth, mercy and righteousness, love and holiness. God's light among us should be reflected in distinctive ways like the following:

A. We believe that human life begins at conception and ends upon natural death, and that all human life is priceless in the eyes of God. All humans should be treated as image-bearers of God. For this reason, we stand for the sanctity of life both at its beginning and its end. We oppose elective abortions and euthanasia as immoral and sinful. We understand that there are very rare circumstances that may lead to difficult choices when a mother or child's life is at stake, and we prayerfully surrender and defer to God's wisdom, grace, and mercy in those circumstances.
B. We believe God created marriage as the context for the expression and enjoyment of sexual relations. Jesus defines marriage as a covenant between one man and one woman. We believe that all sexual activity outside the bounds of marriage, including same-sex unions and same-sex marriage, are immoral and must not be condoned by disciples of Jesus.

C. We believe that Jesus invites all races and ethnicities into the kingdom of God. Because humanity has exhibited grave racial injustices throughout history, we believe that everyone, especially disciples, must be proactive in securing justice for people of all races and that racial reconciliation must be a priority for the church.

D. We believe that both men and women were created by God to equally reflect, in gendered ways, the nature and character of God in the world. In marriage, husbands and wives are to submit to one another, yet there are gender specific expressions: husbands model themselves in relationship with their wives after Jesus' sacrificial love for the church, and wives model themselves in relationship with their husbands after the church's willingness to follow Jesus. In the church, men and women serve as partners in the use of their gifts in ministry, while seeking to uphold New Testament norms which teach that the lead teacher/preacher role in the gathered church and the elder/overseer role are for qualified men. The vision of the Bible is an equal partnership of men and women in creation, in marriage, in salvation, in the gifts of the Spirit, and in the ministries of the church but exercised in ways that honor gender as described in the Bible.

E. We believe that we must resist the forces of culture that focus on materialism and greed. The Bible teaches that the love of money is the root of all sorts of evil and that greed is idolatry. Disciples of Jesus should joyfully give liberally and work sacrificially for the poor, the marginalized, and the oppressed.

Romans 12:3–8; Matthew 22:36–40; 1 Corinthians 12:4–7; Ephesians 2:10; 4:11–13; 1 Peter 4:10–11; Matthew 20:24–27; Philippians 1:1; Acts 20:28; 1 Timothy 2:11–15; 3:1–7; Titus 1:5–9; 1 Corinthians 11:2–9; 14:33–36; Ephesians 5:21–33; Colossians 3:18–19; 1 Corinthians 7:32–35.

10. *The end.* We believe that Jesus is coming back to earth in order to bring this age to an end. Jesus will reward the saved and punish the wicked, and finally destroy God's last enemy, death. He will put all things under the Father, so that God may be all in all forever. That is why we have urgency for the Great Commission—to make disciples of all nations. We like to look at the Great Commission as an inherent part of God's original command to "be fruitful and multiply."

We want to be disciples of Jesus who love people and help them to be disciples of Jesus. We are a movement of disciples who make disciples who help renew existing churches and who start new churches that make more disciples. We want to reach as many as possible—until Jesus returns and God restores all creation to himself in the new heaven and new earth.

Matthew 25:31–32; Acts 17:31; Revelation 20:11–15; 2 Thessalonians 1:6–10; Mark 9:43–49; Luke 12:4–7; Acts 4:12; John 14:6; Luke 24:46–48; Matthew 28:19–20; Genesis 12:1–3; Galatians 2:20; 4:19; Luke 6:40; Luke 19:10; Revelation 21:1ff.

NOTES

1. The grammar surrounding the word "spirit" in the Bible is a bit complex. The Old Testament word for "spirit" is a feminine word. Grammatically, a feminine pronoun (she) can be used with the Hebrew word for "spirit," and feminine verbal forms are used with the phrase "Spirit of the Lord" in the Hebrew Old Testament (e.g., Judges 3:10; 1 Samuel 10:6). In the New Testament, the Greek word for "spirit" is neuter, being neither masculine nor feminine. Grammatically, the Greek word should take the pronoun "it." In biblical Hebrew and Greek, however, gender is usually a grammatical construct and not a gendered one. In other words, having a feminine noun for the word "spirit" does not necessarily imply that the Hebrews thought of the Spirit as feminine, and having a neuter noun in Greek does not imply that Greeks thought of the Spirit as non-personal. Since the Spirit is a person and a member of the Godhead, it is proper to refer to the Spirit as "he." To refer to the Spirit as "it" is not wrong, but

this may create confusion about his personal nature. To refer to the Spirit as "she" in English would be misleading, since the English word "spirit" is not feminine (even though the Hebrew word is).

2. Michael Green, *I Believe in the Holy Spirit* (Grand Rapids: Eerdmans, 1975), 18ff. Green argues that *nephesh* generally means the life and consciousness of humans and generally belongs to *us*, while *ruach* denotes a God-like quality in humans that belongs to God and is only loaned to us. Even Green, however, understands that there is considerable overlap in Scripture between the two terms.

3. See Luke 12:55 and 2 Thessalonians 2:8 where verbal forms of *pneuma* are used; see also Jesus' pun on "spirit/wind" in John 3:3–8.

4. Charles Taylor, *A Secular Age* (Cambridge: Belknap Press, 2007).

5. The Bible uses several terms for "the Holy Spirit." The most common is simply "the Spirit" (see Numbers 11:25; 1 Peter 3:18). Also used are the terms "the Spirit of God" (see Genesis 1:2; Matthew 12:28) and "the Spirit of the LORD" (see Judges 3:10; Acts 8:39). The term "Holy Spirit" occurs nearly one hundred times (see Psalm 51:11; Mark 1:8), and the term "Spirit of holiness" occurs once (Romans 1:4). The Spirit is referred to as "the Spirit of the Father" (Matthew 10:20) and "the Spirit of Christ" (Romans 8:9). Paul also declares

"the Lord is the Spirit" (2 Corinthians 3:17). In John's Gospel, Jesus refers to the Spirit as a "Comforter" (Greek = *parakletos*) (John 14:26; 15:26).

6. Craig Keener's book *Miracles: The Credibility of the New Testament Accounts*, 2 vols. (Grand Rapids: Baker Academic, 2011) is helpful here. Keener, an evangelical scholar, documents numerous examples of God doing extraordinary miracles in recent years. See volume 1, pp. 264–358. Add to this the endless number of witnesses who have experienced such miracles, including me personally. One could perhaps easily dismiss a claim about miracles here or there, but when confronted with hundreds of examples, it becomes impossible to say that God is not doing such physics-defying wonders and powers. As G. K. Chesterton once quipped, "Believers in miracles accept them (rightly or wrongly) because they have evidence for them. The disbelievers in miracles deny them (rightly or wrongly) because they have a doctrine against them." *Orthodoxy* (New York: Cosimo Classics, 2007), 143.

7. The dangers of confusing our thoughts with those of the Spirit's has been pointed out by others, including those who insist that a primary work of the Spirit is to illuminate the Word in our hearts. The sixteenth-century reformer John Calvin explained that though we can hear the Spirit-inspired Word of God, the sinfulness of our minds prevents us from believing it without

an inner testimony of God's Spirit. "For the Lord has so knit together the certainty of his word and his Spirit, that our minds are duly imbued with reverence for the word when the Spirit shining upon it enables us there to behold the face of God; and, on the other hand, we embrace the Spirit with no danger of delusion when we recognize him in his image, that is in his word" (John Calvin, *Institutes of the Christian Religion* [Albany: The Ages Digital Library, Version 1.0, 1996], 112). John Wesley speaks of this same work of the Spirit, explaining, "By the testimony of the Spirit, I mean, an inward impression on the soul whereby the Spirit of God immediately and directly witnesses to my spirit, that I am a child of God; that Jesus Christ hath loved me, and given himself for me; that all my sins are blotted out, and I, even I, am reconciled to God" (John Wesley, Sermon Ten: "The Witness of the Spirit," in *The Works of John Wesley*, vol. 5 [Albany: The Ages Digital Library, Version 1.0, 1996], 188). Both Calvin and Wesley were, however, concerned that the doctrine of illumination would one day degenerate into a cheapened concept of intuition or sentiment. Both explicitly warned against following an "inner voice" or one's "inner visions." Calvin chastises those who would "fasten upon any dreaming notion which may have casually sprung up in their minds" as though these notions were from the Spirit (Ibid., 112). And realizing the possible abuses some would make of the doctrine of illumination, Wesley sympathizes with those who might deny any illumination at all. "How many have mistaken the voice of their own imagination for this witness of the Spirit of God, and thence idly presumed they were children of God while they were doing the works of the devil!" (Ibid., 175).

8. For more on what it means to have a biblical faith, see Mark E. Moore, *Faithful Faith: Reclaiming Faith from Culture and Tradition* (Renew.org, 2021).

9. We should not downplay the role of water baptism in the convert's response of faith because water baptism is a normative part of faith in the New Testament. Indeed, the very New Testament that states that we receive the Spirit through faith also says that we receive it through obedience (Acts 5:32). This is not a contradiction, for biblical faith is faithful and obedient. See Tony Twist, Bobby Harrington, and David Young, *Baptism: What the Bible Teaches* (Renew.org, 2019) and David Young, *King Jesus and the Beauty of Obedience Based-Discipleship* (Grand Rapids: Zondervan, 2020).

10. I say "normative" because there are examples in the Bible where the Spirit worked in close connection with a believer's baptism but not at the actual point of baptism. In Acts 8, the Samaritans were baptized in water by Philip but did not receive the Spirit until the arrival of Peter and John. In Acts 10, Cornelius received the Spirit before Peter had even completed his

sermon and shortly before Cornelius's baptism. Both cases appear to be exceptional. In the first, the gospel had made its first crossover from Jews to Samaritans and therefore required an act of the apostles before the Spirit could be received. In the second, the gospel made its first crossover to the Gentiles, and God himself had to pour out the Spirit in order to demonstrate that he wanted Peter to accept Gentile conversions. In fact, it is possible that neither exception refers to receiving the indwelling of the Spirit at all. Rather, it is possible that these exceptions refer to receiving a momentary ecstatic act of the Spirit—such as that which overtook Samson (Judges 13:5) or Saul (1 Samuel 10:11)—neither of whom had the indwelling of the Spirit.

11. In all three Synoptic Gospels, Jesus warned against "blaspheming the Holy Spirit" (Matthew 12:31–37; Mark 3:28–30; Luke 12:10). He stated that such a sin is an "eternal sin" that cannot be forgiven "either in this age or in the age to come." What is the sin against the Holy Spirit, and how does one commit it? In all three Gospels, Jesus' warning was issued in response to the Jewish leaders' accusation that Jesus was driving out demons by the power of Satan. This accusation goes way beyond a rejection of the Savior. Instead, the sin involves accusing the Spirit of being Satan. It strikes at the very root of good and evil and the very nature of the righteousness of God. Jesus' response severely warned that

those who commit this sin will not be forgiven. One should remember, though, that 1 John 1:5–2:4 promises us that the blood of Jesus cleanses "all sin" from those who "walk in the light." In Acts 6:7 and 15:5, Luke even indicates that many Jewish leaders (perhaps even those who earlier had blasphemed) were later converted to Christ. For this reason, we should not understand the sin against the Spirit to be something God refuses to forgive, but rather, we should understand the sin against the Holy Spirit to be any sin so egregious that people refuse to come back to God afterward. These persons leave themselves without any possible application of the redemptive blood of Christ. Living in such a condition leaves one in an unforgivable state. When sinners come to Christ, however, even from such a cut-off position, they can be forgiven. It is only those who will not return who are guilty of the "eternal sin."

12. For an analysis of some of the dangers of claiming the authority of the Twelve, see Douglas Geivett and Holly Pivec, *A New Apostolic Reformation?: A Biblical Response to a Worldwide Movement*, 2nd ed. (Bellington: Lexham Press, 2014).

13. There is considerable disagreement over what the New Testament considers to be prophecy. The typical evangelical view is reflected in the work of C. C. Ryrie, *The Holy Spirit* (Chicago: Moody, 1965). Ryrie believes that all references to prophecy in the New Testament

involve inspired, infallible speech. For Ryrie, this gift is limited only to the first century. Charismatic scholars such as Wayne Grudem distinguish between the kind of prophecy given to the apostles, which was fully inspired and never wrong, from that of ordinary prophets, which carries much less authority and is more analogous to preaching. See Grudem, *The Gift of Prophecy* (Wheaton: Crossway, 1988, 2000). A comprehensive study of the question can be found in Max Turner, *The Holy Spirit and Spiritual Gifts* (Peabody: Hendrickson, 1996).

14. Deuteronomy 13:1–5; 18:22; Isaiah 9:14–15; Jeremiah 6:13; Ezekiel 22:28; Micah 2:11; 3:11; Matthew 7:15; 24:11, 24; Acts 13:6; 1 Corinthians 12:3; Galatians 1:6–9; 2 Peter 2:1; 1 John 4:6.

15. John Kildahl was a clinical psychologist who devoted ten years to the study of idiolalia. He concluded that it is not any known language, even though it has fluidity, rhythm, and feeling. Idiolalia, he explains, has no fixed or shared meaning, which explains why interpreters of idiolalia typically don't agree on what any given idiolalia act means. Kildahl describes idiolalia as "psychological regression," by which he means "a reversion to an earlier level of maturity, during which the rational, common-sense, ego-controlled way of relating to life is somehow diminished. It is perhaps more childlike, less critical, and generally more free-floating in its nature" (*The Psychology of Speaking in Tongues* (New York:

Harper and Row, 1972), 59. The phenomenon occurs in other religions as well (Tibetan Buddhist monks, Muslims, animists, Eskimos, even early Hellenistic religions). Idiolalia even occurs outside of religious circles. For example, the fascinating music of Australian artist Lisa Gerrard often employs idiolalia, which, Gerrard explains, she invented in her teen years to express the inexpressible.

16. Christopher Dana Lynn; Jason Paris; Cheryl Anne Frye; and Lawrence Schell, "Salivary Alpha-Amylase and Cortisol Among Pentecostals on a Worship and Nonworship Day," *American Journal of Human Biology*, vol. 22 (2010: 6): 819–822.

17. Frederick Dale Bruner published a comprehensive study of whether the Pentecostal movement's claims about the miraculous gifts of the Spirit could be justified by the Scriptures, generally concluding that they could not. See *A Theology of the Holy Spirit: The Pentecostal Experience and the New Testament Witness* (Grand Rapids: Eerdmans, 1970). One of Bruner's primary objections to the Pentecostal movement was its belief that such gifts were necessary to validate one's salvation, which clearly goes beyond the text of the Scriptures, dangerously adding to the process of salvation articulated in the New Testament. Contrary to Bruner's thesis, however, a wrongly understood claim to miracles doesn't mean that the Holy Spirit has ceased to give gifts to

believers. It only means that contemporary churches can grossly misunderstand these gifts. More recent teachings by charismatic churches have largely corrected the concerns that Bruner raises.